From a Bushman Cave Drawing
(see page 76)

"Nature demands with no uncertain voice," writes the author, "that the physical needs of the body shall be satisfied first ; but we feel that our real human life only begins where that is accomplished, that the man who works at some uncreative and uncongenial toil merely to earn enough food to enable him to continue to work has not, properly speaking, a human life at all. . . .

"ART both stimulates and controls those indefinable overtones of the material life of man which all of us at moments feel to have a quality of permanence and reality that does not belong to the rest of our experience."

That is what this book is about : that part of man's activities not immediately concerned with the struggle for existence. An idea of the scope of the book may be gathered from the list of subjects dealt with : Art and Life, Art and Socialism, Art and Science, The Art of the Bushmen, Negro Sculpture, Ancient American Art, Mohammedan Art, Giotto, Dürer, El Greco, Blake, Claude, Cézanne, Renoir, The Artist's Vision, etc.

"It is long since we have come across a book so stimulating."—*Daily Chronicle.*

PELICAN BOOKS

Advisory Editors : H. L. BEALES, Reader in Economic History, University of London; W. E. WILLIAMS, Secretary, the British Institute of Adult Education.

VISION AND DESIGN

BY ROGER FRY

PELICAN BOOKS

VISION AND DESIGN

BY

ROGER FRY

PUBLISHED BY

PENGUIN BOOKS LIMITED

HARMONDSWORTH MIDDLESEX ENGLAND

3 EAST 17th STREET NEW YORK U.S.A.

First published December 1920
Fourth printing (revised) March 1925
First issued in the Phoenix Library 1928
Reprinted 1929
Published in Pelican Books 1937
Reprinted JANUARY 1940

MADE AND PRINTED IN GREAT BRITAIN FOR PENGUIN BOOKS LIMITED
BY PURNELL AND SONS, LTD., PAULTON (SOMERSET) AND LONDON

PREFACE

This book contains a selection from my writings on Art extending over a period of twenty years. Some essays have never before been published in England; and I have also added a good deal of new matter and made slight corrections throughout. In the laborious work of hunting up lost and forgotten publications, and in the work of selection, revision, and arrangement I owe everything to Mr. R. R. Tatlock's devoted and patient labour.

R. F.

CONTENTS

VISION AND DESIGN

ART AND LIFE[1]

WHEN we look at ancient works of art we habitually
treat them not merely as objects of æsthetic enjoyment
but also as successive deposits of the human imagination. It is indeed this view of works of art as crystallised
history that accounts for much of the interest felt in
ancient art by those who have but little æsthetic feeling
and who find nothing to interest them in the work of
their contemporaries, where the historical motive is
lacking, and they are left face to face with bare æsthetic
values.

I once knew an old gentleman who had retired from
his city office to a country house—a fussy, feeble, little
being, who had cut no great figure in life. He had
built himself a house which was preternaturally hideous;
his taste was deplorable and his manners indifferent;
but he had a dream, the dream of himself as an exquisite
and refined intellectual dandy living in a society of
elegant frivolity. To realise this dream he had spent
large sums in buying up every scrap of eighteenth-
century French furniture which he could lay hands on.
These he stored in an immense upper floor in his house,
which was always locked except when he went up to
indulge in his dream and to become for a time a courtier
at Versailles doing homage on the du Barry, whose
toilet-tables and whatnots were strewn pell-mell about
the room without order or effect of any kind. Such is
an extreme instance of the historical way of looking
at works of art. For this old gentleman, as for how

[1] From notes of a lecture given to the Fabian Society, 1917.

11

many an American millionaire, art was merely a help
to an imagined dream life.

To many people then it seems an easy thing to pass
thus directly from the work of art to the life of the
time which produced it. We all in fact weave an
imagined Middle Ages around the parish church and
an imagined Renaissance haunts us in the college
courts of Oxford and Cambridge. We don't, I fancy,
stop to consider very closely how true the imagined
life is: we are satisfied with the prospect of another
sort of life which we might have lived, which we often
think we might have preferred to our actual life. We
don't stop to consider much how far the pictured past
corresponds to any reality, certainly not to consider
what proportion of the whole reality of the past life
gets itself embalmed in this way in works of art. Thus
we picture our Middle Ages as almost entirely occupied
with religion and war, our Renaissance as occupied in
learning, and our eighteenth century as occupied
in gallantry and wit. Whereas, as a matter of fact,
all of these things were going on all the time while
the art of each period has for some reason been mainly
taken up with the expression of one or another activity.
There is indeed a certain danger in accepting too naïvely
the general atmosphere—the ethos, which the works
of art of a period exhale. Thus when we look at the
thirteenth-century sculpture of Chartres or Beauvais we
feel at once the expression of a peculiar gracious piety,
a smiling and gay devoutness which we are tempted to
take for the prevailing mood of the time—and which we
perhaps associate with the revelation of just such a type
of character in S. Francis of Assisi. A study of Salimbeni's
chronicle with its interminable record of squalid avarice
and meanness, or of the fierce brutalities of Dante's Inferno is a necessary corrective of such a pleasant dream.

It would seem then that the correspondence between
art and life which we so habitually assume is not at

all constant and requires much correction before it can
be trusted. Let us approach the same question from
another point and see what result we obtain. Let us
consider the great revolutions in art and the revolutions
in life and see if they coincide. And here let me try
to say what I mean by life as contrasted with art. I
mean the general intellectual and instinctive reaction to
their surroundings of those men of any period whose
lives rise to complete self-consciousness. Their view of
the universe as a whole and their conception of their
relations to their kind. Of course their conception of the
nature and function of art will itself be one of the most
varying aspects of life and may in any particular period
profoundly modify the correspondence of art to life.

Perhaps the greatest revolution in life that we know
of at all intimately was that which effected the change
from Paganism to Christianity. That this was no mere
accident is evident from the fact that Christianity was
only one of many competing religions, all of which
represented a closely similar direction of thought and
feeling. Any one of these would have produced prac-
tically the same effect, that of focusing men's minds
on the spiritual life as opposed to the material life
which had preoccupied them for so long. One cannot
doubt then that here was a change which denoted a
long prepared and inevitable readjustment of men's
attitude to their universe. Now the art of the Roman
Empire showed no trace whatever of this influence; it
went on with precisely the same motives and principles
which had satisfied Paganism. The subjects changed
and became mainly Christian, but the treatment was
so exactly similar that it requires more than a cursory
glance to say if the figure on a sarcophagus is Christ
or Orpheus, Moses or Æsculapius.

The next great turning-point in history is that which
marks the triumph of the forces of reaction towards
the close of the twelfth century—a reaction which

destroyed the promising hopes of freedom of thought
and manners which make the twelfth century appear
as a foretaste of modern enlightenment. Here undoubtedly the change in life corresponds very closely
with a great change in art—the change from the
Romanesque to the Gothic, and at first sight we might
suppose a causal connection between the two. But
when we consider the nature of the changes in the two
sequences, this becomes very doubtful. For whereas in
the life of the Middle Ages the change was one of
reaction—the sharp repression by the reactionary forces
of a gradual growth of freedom—the change in art is
merely the efflorescence of certain long prepared and
anticipated effects. The forms of Gothic architecture
were merely the answer to certain engineering problems
which had long occupied the inventive ingenuity of
twelfth-century architects, while in the figurative arts
the change merely showed a new self-confidence in the
rendering of the human figure, a newly developed
mastery in the handling of material. In short, the
change in art was in the opposite direction to that in
life. Whereas in life the direction of movement was
sharply bent backwards, in art the direction followed
on in a continuous straight line.

It is true that in one small particular the reaction
did have a direct effect on art. The preaching of
S. Bernard of Clairvaux did impose on the architects
who worked for the Cistercian order a peculiar architectural hypocrisy. They were bound by his traditional
influence to make their churches have an appearance of
extreme simplicity and austerity, but they wanted
nevertheless to make them as magnificent and imposing
as possible. The result was a peculiar style of ostentatious
simplicity. Paray le Monial is the only church left
standing in which this curious and, in point of fact,
depressing evidence of the direct influence of the religious
reaction on art is to be seen, and, as a curiosity in

psychological expression, it is well worth a visit. For the rest the movement of art went on entirely unaffected by the new orientation of thought.

We come now to the Renaissance, and here for the first time in our survey we may, I think, safely admit a true correspondence between the change in life and the change in art. The change in life, if one may generalise on such a vast subject, was towards the recognition of the rights of the individual, towards complete self-realisation and the recognition of the objective reality of the material universe which implied the whole scientific attitude—and in both these things the exemplar which men put before themselves was the civilisation of Greece and Rome. In art the change went *pari passu* with the change in life, each assisting and directing the other—the first men of science were artists like Brunelleschi, Ucello, Piero della Francesca and Leonardo da Vinci. The study of classical literature was followed in strict connection with the study of classical canons of art, and the greater sense of individual importance found its expression in the new naturalism which made portraiture in the modern sense possible.

For once then art and the other functions of the human spirit found themselves in perfect harmony and direct alliance, and to that harmony we may attribute much of the intensity and self-assurance of the work of the great Renaissance artists. It is one of the rarest of good fortunes for an artist to find himself actually understood and appreciated by the mass of his educated contemporaries, and not only that, but moving alongside of and in step with them towards a similar goal.

The Catholic reaction retarded and impeded the main movement of Renaissance thought, but it did not really succeed either in suppressing it or changing the main direction of its current. In art it undoubtedly had some direct effect, it created a new kind of insincerity of expression, a florid and sentimental religiosity

—a new variety of bad taste, the rhetorical and over-emphatic. And I suspect that art was already prepared for this step by a certain exhaustion of the impulsive energy of the Renaissance—so that here too we may admit a correspondence.

The seventeenth century shows us no violent change in life, but rather the gradual working out of the principles implicit in the Renaissance and the Catholic reaction. But here we come to another curious want of correspondence between art and life, for in art we have a violent revolution, followed by a bitter inter-necine struggle among artists. This revolution was inaugurated by Caravaggio, who first discovered the surprising emotional possibilities of chiaroscuro and who combined with this a new idea of realism—realism in the modern sense, viz., the literal acceptance of what is coarse, common, squalid or undistinguished in life —realism in the sense of the novelists of Zola's time. To Caravaggio's influence we might trace not only a great deal of Rembrandt's art but the whole of that movement in favour of the extravagantly impressive and picturesque, which culminated in the romantic movement of the nineteenth century. Here, then, is another surprising want of correspondence between art and life.

In the eighteenth century we get a curious pheno-menon. Art goes to court, identifies itself closely with a small aristocratic clique, becomes the exponent of their manners and their tastes. It becomes a luxury. It is no longer in the main stream of spiritual and intellectual effort, and this seclusion of art may account for the fact that the next great change in life—the French Revolution and all its accompanying intellectual ferment—finds no serious correspondence in art. We get a change, it is true; the French Republicans believed they were the counterpart of the Romans, and so David had to invent for them that peculiarly distressing type of the ancient Roman—always in heroic attitudes, always immaculate, spotless and with a highly polished 'Mme. Tussaud' surface. By-the-by, I was almost forgetting that we do owe Mme. Tussaud to the French Revolution. But the real movement of art in quite other directions to David—lay in the gradual unfolding of the Romanticist conception of the world—a world of violent emotional effects, of picturesque accidents, of wild nature, and this was a long prepared reaction from the complacent sophistication of eighteenth-century life. It is possible that one may associate this with the general state of mind that produced the Revolution, since both were a revolt against the established order of the eighteenth century; but curiously enough it found its chief ally in the reaction which followed the Revolution, in the neo-Christianism of Chateaubriand and the new sentimental respect for the age of faith—which, incidentally, appeared so much more picturesque than the age of reason.

It would be interesting at this point to consider how far during the nineteenth century reactionary political and religious thought was inspired primarily by æsthetic considerations—a curious instance of the counter-influence of art on life might perhaps be discovered in the devotees of the Oxford Movement. But this would take us too far afield.

The foregoing violently foreshortened view of history and art will show, I hope, that the usual assumption of a direct and decisive connection between life and art is by no means correct. It may, I hope, give pause to those numerous people who have already promised themselves a great new art as a result of the present war, though perhaps it is as well to let them enjoy it in anticipation, since it is, I fancy, the only way in which they are likely to enjoy a great art of any kind. What this survey suggests to me is that if we consider this special spiritual activity of art we find it no doubt open at times to influences from life, but in the main self-contained—we find the rhythmic sequences of change determined much more by its own internal forces—and by the readjustment within it, of its own elements—than by external forces. I admit, of course, that it is always conditioned more or less by economic changes, but these are rather conditions of its existence at all than directive influences. I also admit that under certain conditions the rhythms of life and of art may coincide with great effect on both; but in the main the two rhythms are distinct, and as often as not play against each other.

We have, I hope, gained some experience with which to handle the real subject of my inquiry, the relation of the modern movement in art to life. To understand it we must go back to the impressionist movement, which dates from about 1870. The artists who called themselves impressionists combined two distinct ideas. On the one hand they upheld, more categorically than ever before, the complete detachment of the artistic vision from the values imposed on vision by everyday life—they claimed, as Whistler did in his "10 o'clock," to be pure artists. On the other hand a group of them used this freedom for the quasi-scientific description of new effects of atmospheric colour and atmospheric perspective, thereby endowing painting with a quite new series of colour harmonies, or at least of harmonies which had not been cultivated by European painters for many hundreds of years. They did more than this—the effects thus explored were completely unfamiliar to the ordinary man, whose vision is limited to the mere recognition of objects with a view to the uses of everyday life. He was forced, in looking at their pictures, to accept as artistic representation something very remote from all his previous expectations, and thereby he also acquired in time a new tolerance in his judgments on works of art, a tolerance which was destined to bear a still further strain in succeeding developments.

As against these great advantages which art owes to impressionism we must set the fact that the pseudo-scientific and analytic method of these painters forced artists to accept pictures which lacked design and formal co-ordination to a degree which had never before been permitted. They, or rather some of them, reduced the artistic vision to a continuous patchwork or mosaic of coloured patches without architectural framework or structural coherence. In this, impressionism marked the climax of a movement which had been going on more or less steadily from the thirteenth century—the tendency to approximate the forms of art more and more exactly to the representation of the totality of appearance. When once representation had been pushed to this point where further development was impossible, it was inevitable that artists should turn round and question the validity of the fundamental assumption that art aimed at representation; and the moment the question was fairly posed it became clear that the pseudo-scientific assumption that fidelity to appearance was the measure of art had no logical foundation. From that moment on it became evident that art had arrived at a critical point, and that the greatest revolution in art that had taken place since Græco-Roman impressionism became converted into Byzantine formalism was inevitable. It was this revolution that Cézanne inaugurated and that Gauguin and van Goch continued. There is no need here to give in detail the characteristics of this new movement: they are sufficiently familiar. But we may summarise them as the re-establishment of purely æsthetic criteria in place of the criterion of conformity to appearance—the rediscovery of the principles of structural design and harmony.

The new movement has also led to a new canon of criticism, and this has changed our attitude to the arts of other times and countries. So long as representation was regarded as the end of art, the skill of the artist and his proficiency in this particular feat of representation was regarded with an admiration which was in fact mainly non-æsthetic. With the new indifference to representation we have become much less interested in skill and not at all interested in knowledge. We are thus no longer cut off from a great deal of barbaric and primitive art the very meaning of which escaped the understanding of those who demanded a certain standard of skill in representation before they could give serious consideration to a work of art. In general the effect of the movement has been to render the artist intensely conscious of the æsthetic unity of the work of art, but singularly naïve and simple as regards other considerations.

It remains to be considered whether the life of the past fifty years has shown any such violent reorientation as we have found in the history of modern art. If we look back to the days of Herbert Spencer and Huxley, what changes are there in the general tendencies of life ? The main ideas of rationalism seem to me to have steadily made way—there have been minor counter revolutions, it is true, but the main current of active thought has surely moved steadily along the lines already laid down. I mean that the scientific attitude is more and more widely accepted. The protests of organised religion and of various mysticisms seem to grow gradually weaker and to carry less weight. Hardly any writers or thinkers of first-rate calibre now appear in the reactionary camp. I see, in short, no big change in direction, no evident revulsion of feeling.

None the less I suppose that a Spencer would be impossible now, and that the materialism of to-day is recognisably different from the materialism of Spencer. It would be very much less naïvely self-confident. It would admit far greater difficulties in presenting its picture of the universe than would have occurred to Spencer. The fact is that scepticism has turned on itself and has gone behind a great many of the axioms that seemed self-evident to the earlier rationalists. I do not see that it has at any point threatened the superstructure of the rationalist position, but it has led us to recognise the necessity of a continual revision and reconstruction of these data. Rationalism has become less arrogant and less narrow in its vision. And this is partly due also to the adventure of the scientific spirit into new regions. I refer to all that immense body of study and speculation which starts from Robertson Smith's "Religion of the Israelites." The discovery of natural law in what seemed to earlier rationalists the chaotic fancies and caprices of the human imagination. The assumption that man is a mainly rational animal has given place to the discovery that he is, like other animals, mainly instinctive. This modifies immensely the attitude of the rationalist—it gives him a new charity and a new tolerance. What seemed like the wilful follies of mad or wicked men to the earlier rationalists are now seen to be inevitable responses to fundamental instinctive needs. By observing mankind the man of science has lost his contempt for him. Now this I think has had an important bearing on the new movement in art. In the first place I find something analogous in the new orientation of scientific and artistic endeavour. Science has turned its instruments in on human nature and begun to investigate its fundamental needs, and art has also turned its vision inwards, has begun to work upon the fundamental necessities of man's æsthetic functions.

But besides this analogy, which may be merely accidental and not causal, I think there can be little doubt that the new scientific development—for it is in no sense a revolution—has modified men's attitude to art. To Herbert Spencer, religion was primitive fear of the unknown and art was sexual attraction— he must have contemplated with perfect equanimity, almost with satisfaction, a world in which both these functions would disappear. I suppose that the scientific man of to-day would be much more ready to admit not only the necessity but the great importance of æsthetic feeling for the spiritual existence of man. The general conception of life in the mid-nineteenth century ruled out art as noxious, or at best, a useless frivolity, and above all as a mere survival of more primitive stages of evolution.

On the other hand, the artist of the new movement is moving into a sphere more and more remote from that of the ordinary man. In proportion as art becomes purer the number of people to whom it appeals gets less. It cuts out all the romantic overtones of life which are the usual bait by which men are induced to accept a work of art. It appeals only to the æsthetic sensibility, and that in most men is comparatively weak.

In the modern movement in art, then, as in so many cases in past history, the revolution in art seems to be out of all proportion to any corresponding change in life as a whole. It seems to find its sources, if at all, in what at present seem like minor movements. Whether the difference between the nineteenth and twentieth centuries will in retrospect seem as great in life as they already do in art I cannot guess—at least it is curious to note how much more conscious we are of the change in art than we are of the general change in thought and feeling.

AN ESSAY IN ÆSTHETICS[1]

A CERTAIN painter, not without some reputation at the present day, once wrote a little book on the art he practises, in which he gave a definition of that art so succinct that I take it as a point of departure for this essay.

"The art of painting," says that eminent authority, "is the art of imitating solid objects upon a flat surface by means of pigments." It is delightfully simple, but

[1] New Quarterly, 1909.

prompts the question—Is that all? And, if so, what a deal of unnecessary fuss has been made about it. Now, it is useless to deny that our modern writer has some very respectable authorities behind him. Plato, indeed, gave a very similar account of the affair, and himself put the question—is it then worth while? And, being scrupulously and relentlessly logical, he decided that it was not worth while, and proceeded to turn the artists out of his ideal republic. For all that, the world has continued obstinately to consider that painting was worth while, and though, indeed, it has never quite made up its mind as to what, exactly, the graphic arts did for it, it has persisted in honouring and admiring its painters.

Can we arrive at any conclusions as to the nature of the graphic arts, which will at all explain our feelings about them, which will at least put them into some kind of relation with the other arts, and not leave us in the extreme perplexity, engendered by any theory of mere imitation? For, I suppose, it must be admitted that if imitation is the sole purpose of the graphic arts, it is surprising that the works of such arts are ever looked upon as more than curiosities, or ingenious toys, are ever taken seriously by grown-up people. Moreover, it will be surprising that they have no recognisable affinity with other arts, such as music or architecture, in which the imitation of actual objects is a negligible quantity.

To form such conclusions is the aim I have put before myself in this essay. Even if the results are not decisive, the inquiry may lead us to a view of the graphic arts that will not be altogether unfruitful.

I must begin with some elementary psychology, with a consideration of the nature of instincts. A great many objects in the world, when presented to our senses, put in motion a complex nervous machinery, which ends in some instinctive appropriate action. We see a wild bull in a field; quite without our conscious interference a nervous process goes on, which, unless we interfere forcibly, ends in the appropriate reaction of flight. The nervous mechanism which results in flight causes a certain state of consciousness, which we call the emotion of fear. The whole of animal life, and a great part of human life, is made up of these instinctive reactions to sensible objects, and their accompanying emotions. But man has the peculiar faculty of calling up again in his mind the echo of past experiences of this kind, of going over it again, "in imagination" as we say. He has, therefore, the possibility of a double life; one the actual life, the other the imaginative life. Between these two lives there is this great distinction, that in the actual life the processes of natural selection have brought it about that the instinctive reaction, such, for instance, as flight from danger, shall be the important part of the whole process, and it is towards this that the man bends his whole conscious endeavour. But in the imaginative life no such action is necessary, and, therefore, the whole consciousness may be focused upon the perceptive and the emotional aspects of the experience. In this way we get, in the imaginative life, a different set of values, and a different kind of perception.

We can get a curious side glimpse of the nature of this imaginative life from the cinematograph. This resembles actual life in almost every respect, except that what the psychologists call the conative part of our reaction to sensations, that is to say, the appropriate resultant action is cut off. If, in a cinematograph, we see a runaway horse and cart, we do not have to think either of getting out of the way or heroically interposing ourselves. The result is that in the first place we *see* the event much more clearly; see a number of quite interesting but irrelevant things, which in real life could not struggle into our consciousness, bent, as it would be, entirely upon the problem of our appropriate reaction. I remember seeing in a cinematograph the arrival of a train at a foreign station and the people descending from the carriages; there was no platform, and to my intense surprise I saw several people turn right round after reaching the ground, as though to orientate themselves; an almost ridiculous performance, which I had never noticed in all the many hundred occasions on which such a scene had passed before my eyes in real life. The fact being that at a station one is never really a spectator of events, but an actor engaged in the drama of luggage or prospective seats, and one actually sees only so much as may help to the appropriate action.

In the second place, with regard to the visions of the cinematograph, one notices that whatever emotions are aroused by them, though they are likely to be weaker than those of ordinary life, are presented more clearly to the consciousness. If the scene presented be one of an accident, our pity and horror, though weak, since we know that no one is really hurt, are felt quite purely, since they cannot, as they would in life, pass at once into actions of assistance.

A somewhat similar effect to that of the cinematograph can be obtained by watching a mirror in which a street scene is reflected. If we look at the street itself we are almost sure to adjust ourselves in some way to its actual existence. We recognise an acquaintance, and wonder why he looks so dejected this morning, or become interested in a new fashion in hats—the moment we do that the spell is broken, we are reacting to life itself in however slight a degree, but, in the mirror, it is easier to abstract ourselves completely, and look upon the changing scene as a whole. It then, at once, takes on the visionary quality, and we become true spectators, not selecting what we will see, but seeing everything equally, and thereby we come to notice a number of appearances and relations of appearances, which would have escaped our notice before, owing to that perpetual economising by selection of what impressions we will assimilate, which in life we perform by unconscious processes. The frame of the mirror, then, does to some extent turn the reflected scene from one that belongs to our actual life into one that belongs rather to the imaginative life. The frame of the mirror makes its surface into a very rudimentary work of art, since it helps us to attain to the artistic vision. For that is what, as you will already have guessed, I have been coming to all this time, namely that the work of art is intimately connected with the secondary imaginative life, which all men live to a greater or less extent.

That the graphic arts are the expression of the imaginative life rather than a copy of actual life might be guessed from observing children. Children, if left to themselves, never, I believe, copy what they see, never, as we say, "draw from nature," but express, with a delightful freedom and sincerity, the mental images which make up their own imaginative lives.

Art, then, is an expression and a stimulus of this imaginative life, which is separated from actual life by the absence of responsive action. Now this responsive action implies in actual life moral responsibility. In art we have no such moral responsibility—it presents a life freed from the binding necessities of our actual existence.

What then is the justification for this life of the imagination which all human beings live more or less fully? To the pure moralist, who accepts nothing but ethical values, in order to be justified, it must be shown not only *not* to hinder but actually to forward right action, otherwise it is not only useless but, since it absorbs our energies, positively harmful. To such a one two views are possible, one the Puritanical view at its narrowest, which regards the life of the imagination as no better or worse than a life of sensual pleasure, and therefore entirely reprehensible. The other view is to argue that the imaginative life does subserve morality. And this is inevitably the view taken by moralists like Ruskin, to whom the imaginative life is yet an absolute necessity. It is a view which leads to some very hard special pleading, even to a self-deception which is in itself morally undesirable.

But here comes in the question of religion, for religion is also an affair of the imaginative life, and, though it claims to have a direct effect upon conduct, I do not suppose that the religious person if he were wise would justify religion entirely by its effect on morality, since that, historically speaking, has not been by any means uniformly advantageous. He would probably say that the religious experience was one which corresponded to certain spiritual capacities of human nature, the exercise of which is in itself good and desirable apart from their effect upon actual life. And so, too, I think the artist might if he chose take a mystical attitude, and declare that the fullness and completeness of the imaginative life he leads may correspond to an existence more real and more important than any that we know of in mortal life.

And in saying this, his appeal would find a sympathetic echo in most minds, for most people would, I think, say that the pleasures derived from art were of an altogether different character and more fundamental than merely sensual pleasures, that they did exercise some faculties which are felt to belong to whatever part of us there may be which is not entirely ephemeral and material.

It might even be that from this point of view we should rather justify actual life by its relation to the imaginative, justify nature by its likeness to art. I mean this, that since the imaginative life comes in the course of time to represent more or less what mankind feels to be the completest expression of its own nature, the freest use of its innate capacities, the actual life may be explained and justified by its approximation here and there, however partially and inadequately, to that freer and fuller life.

Before leaving this question of the justification of art, let me put it in another way. The imaginative life of a people has very different levels at different times, and these levels do not always correspond with the general level of the morality of actual life. Thus in the thirteenth century we read of barbarity and cruelty which would shock even us; we may, I think, admit that our moral level, our general humanity is decidedly higher to-day, but the level of our imaginative life is incomparably lower; we are satisfied there with a grossness, a sheer barbarity and squalor which would have shocked the thirteenth century profoundly. Let us admit the moral gain gladly, but do we not also feel a loss; do we not feel that the average business man would be in every way a more admirable, more respectable being if his imaginative life were not so squalid and incoherent? And, if we admit any loss then, there is some function in human nature other than a purely ethical one, which is worthy of exercise.

Now the imaginative life has its own history both in the race and in the individual. In the individual life one of the first effects of freeing experience from the necessities of appropriate responsive action is to indulge recklessly the emotion of self-aggrandisement. The day-dreams of a child are filled with extravagant romances in which he is always the invincible hero. Music—which of all the arts supplies the strongest stimulus to the imaginative life and at the same time has the least power of controlling its direction—music, at certain stages of people's lives, has the effect merely of arousing in an almost absurd degree this egoistic elation, and Tolstoy appears to believe that this is its only possible effect. But with the teaching of experience and the growth of character the imaginative life comes to respond to other instincts and to satisfy other desires, until, indeed, it reflects the highest aspirations and the deepest aversions of which human nature is capable.

In dreams and when under the influence of drugs the imaginative life passes out of our own control, and in such cases its experiences may be highly undesirable, but whenever it remains under our own control it must always be on the whole a desirable life. That is not to say that it is always pleasant, for it is pretty clear that mankind is so constituted as to desire much besides pleasure, and we shall meet among the great artists, the great exponents, that is, of the imaginative life, many to whom the merely pleasant is very rarely a part of what is desirable. But this desirability of the imaginative life does distinguish it very sharply from actual life, and this is the direct result of that first fundamental difference, its freedom from necessary external conditions. Art, then, is, if I am right, the chief organ of the imaginative life; it is by art that it is stimulated and controlled within us, and, as we have seen, the imaginative life is distinguished by the greater clearness of its perception, and the greater purity and freedom of its emotion.

First with regard to the greater clearness of perception. The needs of our actual life are so imperative, that the sense of vision becomes highly specialised in their service. With an admirable economy we learn to see only so much as is needful for our purposes; but this is in fact very little, just enough to recognise and identify each object or person; that done, they go into an entry in our mental catalogue and are no more really seen. In actual life the normal person really only reads the labels as it were on the objects around him and troubles no further. Almost all the things which are useful in any way put on more or less this cap of invisibility. It is only when an object exists

in our lives for no other purpose than to be seen that
we really look at it, as for instance at a China ornament
or a precious stone, and towards such even the most
normal person adopts to some extent the artistic
attitude of pure vision abstracted from necessity.

Now this specialisation of vision goes so far that
ordinary people have almost no idea of what things
really look like, so that oddly enough the one standard
that popular criticism applies to painting, namely,
whether it is like nature or not, is one which most
people are, by the whole tenor of their lives, prevented from applying properly. The only things they
have ever really *looked* at being other pictures; the
moment an artist who has looked at nature brings to
them a clear report of something definitely seen by
him, they are wildly indignant at its untruth to nature.
This has happened so constantly in our own time
that there is no need to prove it. One instance will
suffice. Monet is an artist whose chief claim to recognition lies in the fact of his astonishing power of
faithfully reproducing certain aspects of nature, but
his really naïve innocence and sincerity were taken
by the public to be the most audacious humbug, and
it required the teaching of men like Bastien-Lepage,
who cleverly compromised between the truth and an
accepted convention of what things looked like, to
bring the world gradually round to admitting truths
which a single walk in the country with purely unbiased
vision would have established beyond doubt.

But though this clarified sense perception which
we discover in the imaginative life is of great interest,
and although it plays a larger part in the graphic arts
than in any other, it might perhaps be doubted whether,
interesting, curious, fascinating as it is, this aspect of
the imaginative life would ever by itself make art of
profound importance to mankind. But it is different,
I think, with the emotional aspect. We have admitted

that the emotions of the imaginative are generally weaker than those of actual life. The picture of a saint being slowly flayed alive, revolting as it is, will not produce the same physical sensations of sickening disgust that a modern man would feel if he could assist at the actual event; but they have a compensating clearness of presentment to the consciousness. The more poignant emotions of actual life have, I think, a kind of numbing effect analogous to the paralysing influence of fear in some animals; but even if this experience be not generally admitted, all will admit that the need for responsive action hurries us along and prevents us from ever realising fully what the emotion is that we feel, from co-ordinating it perfectly with other states. In short, the motives we actually experience are too close to us to enable us to feel them clearly. They are in a sense unintelligible. In the imaginative life, on the contrary, we can both feel the emotion and watch it. When we are really moved at the theatre we are always both on the stage and in the auditorium.

Yet another point about the emotions of the imaginative life—since they require no responsive action we can give them a new valuation. In real life we must to some extent cultivate those emotions which lead to useful action, and we are bound to appraise emotions according to the resultant action. So that, for instance, the feelings of rivalry and emulation do get an encouragement which perhaps they scarcely deserve, whereas certain feelings which appear to have a high intrinsic value get almost no stimulus in actual life. For instance, those feelings to which the name of the cosmic emotion has been somewhat unhappily given find almost no place in life, but, since they seem to belong to certain very deep springs of our nature, do become of great importance in the arts.

Morality, then, appreciates emotion by the standard

of resultant action. Art appreciates emotion in and for itself.

This view of the essential importance in art of the expression of the emotions is the basis of Tolstoy's marvellously original and yet perverse and even exasperating book, "What is Art?" and I willingly confess, while disagreeing with almost all his results, how much I owe to him.

He gives an example of what he means by calling art the means of communicating emotions. He says, let us suppose a boy to have been pursued in the forest by a bear. If he returns to the village and merely states that he was pursued by a bear and escaped, that is ordinary language, the means of communicating facts or ideas; but if he describes his state first of heedlessness, then of sudden alarm and terror as the bear appears, and finally of relief when he gets away, and describes this so that his hearers share his emotions, then his description is a work of art.

Now in so far as the boy does this in order to urge the villagers to go out and kill the bear, though he may be using artistic methods, his speech is not a pure work of art; but if of a winter evening the boy relates his experience for the sake of the enjoyment of his adventure in retrospect, or better still, if he makes up the whole story for the sake of the imagined emotions, then his speech becomes a pure work of art. But Tolstoy takes the other view, and values the emotions aroused by art entirely for their reaction upon actual life, a view which he courageously maintains even when it leads him to condemn the whole of Michelangelo, Raphael and Titian, and most of Beethoven, not to mention nearly everything he himself has written, as bad or false art.

Such a view would, I think, give pause to any less heroic spirit. He would wonder whether mankind could have always been so radically wrong about a function that, whatever its value be, is almost universal. And in point of fact he will have to find some other word to denote what we now call art. Nor does Tolstoy's theory even carry him safely through his own book, since, in his examples of morally desirable and therefore good art, he has to admit that these are to be found, for the most part, among works of inferior quality. Here, then, is at once the tacit admission that another standard than morality is applicable. We must therefore give up the attempt to judge the work of art by its reaction on life, and consider it as an expression of emotions regarded as ends in themselves. And this brings us back to the idea we had already arrived at, of art as the expression of the imaginative life.

If, then, an object of any kind is created by man not for use, for its fitness to actual life, but as an object of art, an object subserving the imaginative life, what will its qualities be? It must in the first place be adapted to that disinterested intensity of contemplation, which we have found to be the effect of cutting off the responsive action. It must be suited to that heightened power of perception which we found to result therefrom.

And the first quality that we demand in our sensations will be order, without which our sensations will be troubled and perplexed, and the other quality will be variety, without which they will not be fully stimulated.

It may be objected that many things in nature, such as flowers, possess these two qualities of order and variety in a high degree, and these objects do undoubtedly stimulate and satisfy that clear disinterested contemplation which is characteristic of the æsthetic attitude. But in our reaction to a work of art there is something more—there is the consciousness of purpose, the consciousness of a peculiar relation of sympathy with the man who made this thing in order to arouse precisely the sensations we experience. And

when we come to the higher works of art, where sensations are so arranged that they arouse in us deep
emotions, this feeling of a special tie with the man
who expressed them becomes very strong. We feel
that he has expressed something which was latent
in us all the time, but which we never realised, that
he has revealed us to ourselves in revealing himself.
And this recognition of purpose is, I believe, an essential
part of the æsthetic judgment proper.

The perception of purposeful order and variety
in an object gives us the feeling which we express by
saying that it is beautiful, but when by means of sensations our emotions are aroused we demand purposeful order and variety in them also, and if this can
only be brought about by the sacrifice of sensual
beauty we willingly overlook its absence.

Thus, there is no excuse for a china pot being ugly,
there is every reason why Rembrandt's and Degas'
pictures should be, from the purely sensual point of
view, supremely and magnificently ugly.

This, I think, will explain the apparent contradiction
between two distinct uses of the word beauty, one for
that which has sensuous charm, and one for the
æsthetic approval of works of imaginative art where
the objects presented to us are often of extreme ugliness.
Beauty in the former sense belongs to works of art
where only the perceptual aspect of the imaginative life
is exercised, beauty in the second sense becomes as
it were supersensual, and is concerned with the appropriateness and intensity of the emotions aroused.
When these emotions are aroused in a way that satisfies
fully the needs of the imaginative life we approve and
delight in the sensations through which we enjoy that
heightened experience because they possess purposeful
order and variety in relation to those emotions.

One chief aspect of order in a work of art is unity;
unity of some kind is necessary for our restful con-

templation of the work of art as a whole, since if it lacks unity we cannot contemplate it in its entirety, but we shall pass outside it to other things necessary to complete its unity.

In a picture this unity is due to a balancing of the attractions of the eye about the central line of the picture. The result of this balance of attractions is that the eye rests willingly within the bounds of the picture. Dr. Denman Ross of Harvard University has made a most valuable study of the elementary considerations upon which this balance is based in his "Theory of Pure Design." He sums up his results in the formula that a composition is of value in proportion to the number of orderly connections which it displays.

Dr. Ross wisely restricts himself to the study of abstract and meaningless forms. The moment representation is introduced forms have an entirely new set of values. Thus a line which indicated the sudden bend of a head in a certain direction would have far more than its mere value as line in the composition because of the attraction which a marked gesture has for the eye. In almost all paintings this disturbance of the purely decorative values by reason of the representative effect takes place, and the problem becomes too complex for geometrical proof.

This merely decorative unity is, moreover, of very different degrees of intensity in different artists and in different periods. The necessity for a closely woven geometrical texture in the composition is much greater in heroic and monumental design than in genre pieces on a small scale.

It seems also probable that our appreciation of unity in pictorial design is of two kinds. We are so accustomed to consider only the unity which results from the balance of a number of attractions presented to the eye simultaneously in a framed picture that we forget the possibility of other pictorial forms.

In certain Chinese paintings the length is so great that we cannot take in the whole picture at once, nor are we intended to do so. Sometimes a landscape is painted upon a roll of silk so long that we can only look at it in successive segments. As we unroll it at one end and roll it up at the other we traverse wide stretches of country, tracing, perhaps, all the vicissitudes of a river from its source to the sea, and yet, when this is well done, we have received a very keen impression of pictorial unity.

Such a successive unity is of course familiar to us in literature and music, and it plays its part in the graphic arts. It depends upon the forms being presented to us in such a sequence that each successive element is felt to have a fundamental and harmonious relation with that which preceded it. I suggest that in looking at drawings our sense of pictorial unity is largely of this nature; we feel, if the drawing be a good one, that each modulation of the line as our eye passes along it gives order and variety to our sensations. Such a drawing may be almost entirely lacking in the geometrical balance which we are accustomed to demand in paintings, and yet have, in a remarkable degree, unity.

Let us now see how the artist passes from the stage of merely gratifying our demand for sensuous order and variety to that where he arouses our emotions. I will call the various methods by which this is affected the emotional elements of design.

The first element is that of the rhythm of the line with which the forms are delineated.

The drawn line is the record of a gesture, and that gesture is modified by the artist's feeling which is thus communicated to us directly.

The second element is mass. When an object is so represented that we recognise it as having inertia, we feel its power of resisting movement, or communicating its own movement to other bodies, and our imaginative reaction to such an image is governed by our experience of mass in actual life.

The third element is space. The same-sized square on two pieces of paper can be made by very simple means to appear to represent either a cube two or three inches high, or a cube of hundreds of feet, and our reaction to it is proportionately changed.

The fourth element is that of light and shade. Our feelings towards the same object become totally different according as we see it strongly illuminated against a black background or dark against light.

A fifth element is that of colour. That this has a direct emotional effect is evident from such words as gay, dull, melancholy in relation to colour.

I would suggest the possibility of another element, though perhaps it is only a compound of mass and space: it is that of the inclination to the eye of a plane, whether it is impending over or leaning away from us.

Now it will be noticed that nearly all these emotional elements of design are connected with essential conditions of our physical existence: rhythm appeals to all the sensations which accompany muscular activity; mass to all the infinite adaptations to the force of gravity which we are forced to make; the spatial judgment is equally profound and universal in its application to life; our feeling about inclined planes is connected with our necessary judgments about the conformation of the earth itself; light again, is so necessary a condition of our existence that we become intensely sensitive to changes in its intensity. Colour is the only one of our elements which is not of critical or universal importance to life, and its emotional effect is neither so deep nor so clearly determined as the others. It will be seen, then, that the graphic arts arouse emotions in us by playing upon what one may call the overtones of some of our primary physical needs. They have, indeed, this great advantage over poetry, that they can appeal more directly and immediately to the emotional accompaniments of our bare physical existence.

If we represent these various elements in simple diagrammatic terms, this effect upon the emotions is, it must be confessed, very weak. Rhythm of line, for instance, is incomparably weaker in its stimulus of the muscular sense than is rhythm addressed to the ear in music, and such diagrams can at best arouse only faint ghost-like echoes of emotions of differing qualities; but when these emotional elements are combined with the presentation of natural appearances, above all with the appearance of the human body, we find that this effect is indefinitely heightened.

When, for instance, we look at Michelangelo's "Jeremiah," and realise the irresistible momentum his movements would have, we experience powerful sentiments of reverence and awe. Or when we look at Michelangelo's "Tondo" in the Uffizi, and find a group of figures so arranged that the planes have a sequence comparable in breadth and dignity to the mouldings of the earth mounting by clearly-felt gradations to an overtopping summit, innumerable instinctive reactions are brought into play.[1]

At this point the adversary (as Leonardo da Vinci calls him) is likely enough to retort, "You have abstracted from natural forms a number of so-called emotional elements which you yourself admit are very weak when stated with diagrammatic purity; you then put them back, with the help of Michelangelo, into the natural forms whence they were derived, and at once they have value, so that after all it appears that the natural forms contain these emotional elements ready made up for us, and all that art need do is to imitate Nature."

[1] Rodin is reported to have said, "A woman, a mountain, a horse—they are all the same thing; they are made on the same principles." That is to say, their forms, when viewed with the disinterested vision of the imaginative life, have similar emotional elements.

But, alas! Nature is heartlessly indifferent to the needs of the imaginative life; God causes His rain to fall upon the just and upon the unjust. The sun neglects to provide the appropriate limelight effect even upon a triumphant Napoleon or a dying Cæsar.[1] Assuredly we have no guarantee that in nature the emotional elements will be combined appropriately with the demands of the imaginative life, and it is, I think, the great occupation of the graphic arts to give us first of all order and variety in the sensuous plane, and then so to arrange the sensuous presentment of objects that the emotional elements are elicited with an order and appropriateness altogether beyond what Nature herself provides.

Let me sum up for a moment what I have said about the relation of art to Nature, which is, perhaps, the greatest stumbling-block to the understanding of the graphic arts.

I have admitted that there is beauty in Nature, that is to say, that certain objects constantly do, and perhaps any object may, compel us to regard it with that intense disinterested contemplation that belongs to the imaginative life, and which is impossible to the actual life of necessity and action; but that in objects created to arouse the æsthetic feeling we have an added consciousness of purpose on the part of the creator, that he made it on purpose not to be used but to be regarded and enjoyed; and that this feeling is characteristic of the æsthetic judgment proper.

When the artist passes from pure sensations to emotions aroused by means of sensations, he uses natural forms which, in themselves, are calculated to move our emotions, and he presents these in such a manner that the forms themselves generate in us emotional states, based upon the fundamental neces-

[1] I do not forget that at the death of Tennyson the writer in the *Daily Telegraph* averred that "level beams of the setting moon streamed in upon the face of the dying bard"; but then, after all, in its way the *Daily Telegraph* is a work of art.

sities of our physical and physiological nature. The artist's attitude to natural form is, therefore, infinitely various according to the emotions he wishes to arouse. He may require for his purpose the most complete representation of a figure, he may be intensely realistic, provided that his presentment, in spite of its closeness to natural appearance, disengages clearly for us the appropriate emotional elements. Or he may give us the merest suggestion of natural forms, and rely almost entirely upon the force and intensity of the emotional elements involved in his presentment.

We may, then, dispense once for all with the idea of likeness to Nature, of correctness or incorrectness as a test, and consider only whether the emotional elements inherent in natural form are adequately discovered, unless, indeed, the emotional idea depends at any point upon likeness, or completeness of representation.

THE OTTOMAN AND THE WHATNOT[1]

SUCH were the outlandish names of the two great clans that marched under the flag of the Antimacassar to the resounding periods of Mr. Podsnap's rhetoric. For all the appearance of leisure, for all the absence of hustle, those were strenuous days. Respectability and "the young person" were perpetually menaced by inveterate human nature, and were always or nearly always just being saved as by a miracle. But in the end it was the boast of the Victorians that they had established a system of taboos almost as complicated and as all-pervading as that of the Ojibbeways or the Waramunga. The Ottoman, which seated two so conveniently, was liable to prove a traitor, but what the Ottoman risked could be saved by the Whatnot, with Tennyson and John Greenleaf Whittier to counsel

[1] Athenæum, 1919.

and assuage. One of the things they used to say in those days, quite loudly and distinctly, was: "Distance lends enchantment to the view." It seemed so appropriate at the frequent and admirably organised picnics that at last it was repeated too often, and the time came when, under pain of social degradation, it was forbidden to utter the hated words. But now that we are busy bringing back the Ottoman and the Whatnot from the garret and the servants' hall to the drawing-room, we may once more repeat the phrase with impunity, and indeed this article has no other purpose than to repeat once more (and with how new a relish !): "Distance lends enchantment to the view."

Also, with our passion for science and exact measurement, we shall wish to discover the exact distance at which enchantment begins. And this is easier than might be supposed; for any one who has lived long enough will have noticed that a certain distance lends a violent disgust to the view—that as we recede there comes a period of oblivion and total unconsciousness, to be succeeded when consciousness returns by the ecstasy, the nature of which we are considering.

I, alas ! can remember the time when the Ottoman and Whatnot still lingered in the drawing-rooms of the less fashionable and more conservative bourgeoisie; lingered despised, rejected, and merely awaiting their substitutes. I can remember the sham Chippendale and the sham old oak which replaced them. I can remember a still worse horror—a genuine modern style which as yet has no name, a period of black polished wood with spidery lines of conventional flowers incised in the wood and then gilt. These things must have belonged to the 'eighties—I think they went with the bustle; but as they are precisely at the distance where unconsciousness has set in, it is more difficult to me to write the history of this period than it would be to tell of the sequence of styles in the Tang dynasty. And now, having watched the Whatnot disappear, I have the privilege of watching its resurrection. I have passed from disgust, through total forgetfulness, into the joys of retrospection.

Now my belief is that none of these feelings have anything to do with our æsthetic reactions to the objects as works of art. The odd thing about either real or would-be works of art, that is to say, about any works made with something beyond a purely utilitarian aim—the odd thing is that they can either affect our æsthetic sensibilities or they can become symbols of a particular way of life. In this aspect they affect our historical imagination through our social emotions. That the historical images they conjure up in us are probably false has very little to do with it; the point is that they exist for us, and exist for most people, far more vividly and poignantly than any possible æsthetic feelings. And somehow the works of each period come to stand for us as symbols of some particular and special aspect of life. A Limoges casket evokes the idea of a life of chivalrous adventure and romantic devotion; an Italian cassone gives one a life of intellectual ferment and Boccaccian freedom; before a Caffieri bronze or a Riesener bureau one imagines oneself an exquisite aristocrat proof against the deeper passions, and gifted with a sensuality so refined and a wit so ready that gallantry would be a sufficient occupation for a lifetime. Who ever, handling a Louis XV. tabatière, reflected how few of the friends of its original owner ever washed, and how many of them were marked with small-pox? The fun of these historical evocations is precisely in what they leave out.

And in order that this process of selection and elimination may take place, precise and detailed knowledge must have faded from the collective memory, and the blurred but exquisite outlines of a generalisation must have been established.

We have just got to this point with the Victorian

epoch. It has just got its vague and generalised *Stimmung*. We think as we look at Leech's drawings, or sit in a beadwork chair, of a life which was the perfect flower of bourgeoisie. The aristocracy with their odd irregular ways, the Meredith heroines and heroes, are away in the background; *the* Victorian life is of the upper bourgeoisie. It is immensely leisured, untroubled by social problems, unblushingly sentimental, impenitently unintellectual, and devoted to sport. The women are exquisitely trained to their social functions; they respond unfailingly to every sentimental appeal; they are beautifully ill-informed, and yet yearning for instruction; they have adorable tempers and are ever so mildly mischievous. The men can afford, without fear of impish criticism, to flaunt their whiskers in the sea breeze, and to expatiate on their contempt for everything that is not correct.

Here, I suppose, is something like the outline of that generalised historical fancy that by now emanates so fragrantly from the marble inlaid tables and the beadwork screens of the period. How charming and how false it is, one sees at once when one reflects that we imagine the Victorians for ever playing croquet without ever losing their tempers.

It is evident, then, that we have just arrived at the point where our ignorance of life in the Victorian period is such as to allow the incurable optimism of memory to build a quite peculiar little earthly paradise out of the boredoms, the snobberies, the cruel repressions, the mean calculations and rapacious speculations of the mid-nineteenth century. Go a little later, and the imagination is hopelessly hampered by familiarity with the facts of life which the roseate mist has not yet begun to transmute. But let those of us who are hard at work collecting Victorian paper-weights, stuffed humming-birds and wax flowers reflect that our successors will be able to create quite as amusing and wonderful interiors out of the black wood cabinets and "æsthetic" crewel-work of the 'eighties. They will not be able to do this until they have constructed the appropriate social picture, the outlines of which we cannot yet even dimly conceive. We have at this moment no inkling of the kind of lies they will invent about the 'eighties to amuse themselves; we only know that when the time comes the legend will have taken shape, and that, from that moment on, the objects of the time will have the property of emanation.

So far it has been unnecessary even to consider whether the objects of the Victorian period are works of art or not; all that is necessary is that they should have some margin of freedom from utility, some scope for the fancy of their creators. And the Victorian epoch is, I think, unusually rich in its capacity for emanation, for it was the great period of *fancy work*. As the age-long traditions of craftsmanship and structural design, which had lingered on from the Middle Ages, finally faded out under the impact of the new industrialism, the amateur stepped in, his brain teeming with fancies. Craftsmanship was dead, the craftsman replaced either by the machine or by a purely servile and mechanical human being, a man without tradition, without ideas of his own, who was ready to accomplish whatever caprices the amateur or the artist might set him to. It was an age of invention and experiment, an age of wildly irresponsible frivolity, curiosity and sentimentality. To gratify sentiment, nature was opposed to the hampering conventions of art; to gratify fatuous curiosity, the most improbable and ill-suited materials conceivable were used. What they call in France *le style coco* is exactly expressive of this. A drawing of a pheasant is coloured by cutting up little pieces of real pheasant's feathers and sticking them on in the appropriate places. Realistic flowers are made out of shells glued together, or, with less of the pleasant shock of the unexpected, out of wax or spun glass. They experiment in colour, using the new results of chemistry boldly, greens from arsenic, magenta and maroons from coal-tar, with results sometimes happy, sometimes disastrous; but always we feel behind everything the capricious fancy of the amateur with his desire to contribute by some joke or conjuring trick to the social amenities. The general groundwork of design, so far as any tradition remains at all, is a kind of bastard baroque passing at times into a flimsy caricature of rococo, but almost always so overlaid and transfigured by the fancies of the amateur as to be hardly recognisable, and yet all, by now, so richly redolent of its social legend as to have become a genuine style.

There is reason enough, then, why we should amuse ourselves by collecting Victorian objects of art, or at least those of us who have the special social-historical sensibility highly developed. But so curiously intertwisted are our emotions that we are always apt to put a wrong label on them, and the label "beauty" comes curiously handy for almost any of the more spiritual and disinterested feelings. So our collector is likely enough to ask us to admire his objects, not for their social emanations, but for their intrinsic æsthetic merit, which, to tell the truth, is far more problematical. Certain it is that the use of material at this period seems to be less discriminating, and the sense of quality feebler, than at any previous period of the world's history, at all events since Roman times— Pompeii, by-the-by, was a thoroughly Victorian city. The sense of design was also chaotically free from all the limitations of purpose and material, and I doubt if it attained to that perfect abstract sense of harmony which might justify any disregard of those conditions. No, on the whole it will be better to recognise fully how endearing, how fancy-free, how richly evocative are the objects of the Victorian period than to trouble our heads about their æsthetic value.

The discovery of Victorian art is due to a few enterprising and original artists. In a future article I hope to show why it is to the artist rather than to the collector that we always owe such discoveries, and also why artists are of all people the most indifferent to the æsthetic value of the objects they recommend to our admiration.

THE ARTIST'S VISION[1]

IN the preceding article I stated that artists always lead the way in awakening a new admiration for forgotten and despised styles, and that in doing so they anticipate both the archæologist and the collector. I also suggested that they were of all people the least fitted to report upon the æsthetic value of the objects they pressed upon us.

Biologically speaking, art is a blasphemy. We were given our eyes to see things, not to look at them. Life takes care that we all learn the lesson thoroughly, so that at a very early age we have acquired a very considerable ignorance of visual appearances. We have learned the meaning-for-life of appearances so well that we understand them, as it were, in shorthand. The subtlest differences of appearance that have a utility value still continue to be appreciated, while large and important visual characters, provided they are useless for life, will pass unnoticed. With all the ingenuity and resource which manufacturers put into their business, they can scarcely prevent the ordinary eye from seizing on the minute visual characteristics that distinguish margarine from butter. Some of us can tell Canadian cheddar at a glance, and no one was ever taken in by sham suède gloves.

[1] Athenæum, 1919.

The sense of sight supplies prophetic knowledge of what may affect the inner fortifications, the more intimate senses of taste and touch, where it may already be too late to avert disaster. So we learn to read the prophetic message, and, for the sake of economy, to neglect all else. Children have not learned it fully, and so they look at things with some passion. Even the grown man keeps something of his unbiological, disinterested vision with regard to a few things. He still looks at flowers, and does not merely see them. He also keeps objects which have some marked peculiarity of appearance that catches his eye. These may be natural, like precious stones, fossils, incrustations and such like; or they may be manufactured entirely with a view to pleasing by peculiarities of colour or shape, and these are called ornaments. Such articles, whether natural or artificial, are called by those who sell them "curios," and the name is not an unhappy one to denote the kind of interest which they arouse. As I showed in a previous article, such objects get attached to them a secondary interest, arising from the kind of social milieu that they were made for, so that they become not merely curious for the eye, but stimulating to our social-historical imagination.

The vision with which we regard such objects is quite distinct from the practical vision of our instinctive life. In the practical vision we have no more concern after we have read the label on the object; vision ceases the moment it has served its biological function. But the curiosity vision does contemplate the object disinterestedly; the object *ex hypothesi* has no significance for actual life; it is a play or fancy object, and our vision dwells much more consciously and deliberately upon it. We notice to some extent its forms and colours, especially when it is new to us.

But human perversity goes further even than this in its misapplication of the gift of sight. We may look at objects not even for their curiosity or oddity, but for their harmony of form and colour. To arouse such a vision the object must be more than a "curio": it has to be a work of art. I suspect that such an object must be made by some one in whom the impulse was not to please others, but to express a feeling of his own. It is probably this fundamental difference of origin between the "curio" or ornament and the work of art that makes it impossible for any commercial system, with its eye necessarily on the customer, ever to produce works of art, whatever the ingenuity with which it is attempted.

But we are concerned here not with the origin, but with the vision. This is at once more intense and more detached from the passions of the instinctive life than either of the kinds of vision hitherto discussed. Those who indulge in this vision are entirely absorbed in apprehending the relation of forms and colour to one another, as they cohere within the object. Suppose, for example, that we are looking at a Sung bowl; we apprehend gradually the shape of the outside contour, the perfect sequence of the curves, and the subtle modifications of a certain type of curve which it shows; we also feel the relation of the concave curves of the inside to the outside contour; we realise that the precise thickness of the walls is consistent with the particular kind of matter of which it is made, its appearance of density and resistance; and finally we recognise, perhaps, how satisfactory for the display of all these plastic qualities are the colour and the dull lustre of the glaze. Now while we are thus occupied there comes to us, I think, a feeling of purpose; we feel that all these sensually logical conformities are the outcome of a particular feeling, or of what, for want of a better word, we call an idea; and we may even say that the pot is the expression of an idea in the artist's mind. Whether we are right or not in making this deduction, I believe it nearly always occurs in such æsthetic apprehension of an object of art. But in all this no element of curiosity, no reference to actual life, comes in; our apprehension is unconditioned by considerations of space or time; it is irrelevant to us to know whether the bowl was made seven hundred years ago in China, or in New York yesterday. We may, of course, at any moment switch off from the æsthetic vision, and become interested in all sorts of quasi-biological feelings; we may inquire whether it is genuine or not, whether it is worth the sum given for it, and so forth; but in proportion as we do this we change the focus of our vision; we are more likely to examine the bottom of the bowl for traces of marks than to look at the bowl itself.

Such, then, is the nature of the æsthetic vision, the vision with which we contemplate works of art. It is to such a vision, if to anything outside himself, that the artist appeals, and the artist in his spare hours may himself indulge in the æsthetic vision; and if one can get him to do so, his verdict is likely to be as good as any one's.

The artist's main business in life, however, is carried on by means of yet a fourth kind of vision, which I will call the creative vision. This, I think, is the furthest perversion of the gifts of nature of which man is guilty. It demands the most complete detachment from any of the meanings and implications of appearances. Almost any turn of the kaleidoscope of nature may set up in the artist this detached and impassioned vision, and, as he contemplates the particular field of vision, the (æsthetically) chaotic and accidental conjunction of forms and colours begins to crystallise into a harmony; and as this harmony becomes clear to the artist, his actual vision becomes distorted by the emphasis of the rhythm which has been set up within him. Certa n relations of directions of line become for him full of meaning; he apprehends them no longer casually or merely curiously, but passionately, and these lines begin to be so stressed and stand out so clearly from the rest that he sees them far more distinctly than he did at first. Similarly colours, which in nature have almost always a certain vagueness and elusiveness, become so definite and clear to him, owing to their now necessary relation to other colours, that if he chooses to paint his vision he can state them positively and definitely. In such a creative vision the objects as such tend to disappear, to lose their separate unities, and to take their places as so many bits in the whole mosaic of vision. The texture of the whole field of vision becomes so close that the coherence of the separate patches of tone and colour within each object is no stronger than the coherence with every other tone and colour throughout the field.

In such circumstances the greatest object of art becomes of no more significance than any casual piece of matter; a man's head is no more and no less important than a pumpkin, or, rather, these things may be so or not according to the rhythm that obsesses the artist and crystallises his vision. Since it is the habitual practice of the artist to be on the look-out for these peculiar arrangements of objects that arouse the creative vision, and become material for creative contemplation, he is liable to look at all objects from this point of view. In so far as the artist looks at objects only as part of a whole field of vision which is his own potential picture, he can give no account of their æsthetic value. Every solid object is subject to the play of light and shade, and becomes a mosaic of visual patches, each of which for the artist is related to other visual patches in the surroundings. It is irrelevant to ask him, while he is looking with this generalised and all-embracing vision, about the nature of the objects which compose it. He is likely even to turn away from works of art in which he may be tempted to relapse into an æsthetic vision, and so see them as unities apart from their surroundings. By preference he turns to objects which

make no strong æsthetic appeal in themselves. But
he may like objects which attract by some oddity or
peculiarity of form or colour, and thereby suggest to
him new and intriguing rhythms. In his continual and
restless preoccupation with appearance he is capable
of looking at objects from which both the æsthetic
and even the curious vision would turn away instinctively, or which they may never notice, so little prospect
of satisfaction do they hold out. But the artist may
always find his satisfaction, the material for his picture,
in the most unexpected quarters. Objects of the most
despised periods, or objects saturated for the ordinary
man with the most vulgar and repulsive associations,
may be grist to his mill. And so it happened that while
the man of culture and the connoisseur firmly believed
that art ended with the brothers Adam, Mr. Walter
Sickert was already busy getting hold of stuffed birds
and wax flowers just for his own queer game of tones
and colours. And now the collector and the art-dealer
will be knocking at Mr. Sickert's door to buy the
treasures at twenty times the price the artist paid for
them. Perhaps there are already younger artists who
are getting excited about the tiles in the refreshment
room at South Kensington, and, when the social legend
has gathered round the names of Sir Arthur Sullivan
and Connie Gilchrist, will inspire in the cultured a
deep admiration for the "æsthetic" period.

The artist is of all men the most constantly observant
of his surroundings, and the least affected by their
intrinsic æsthetic value. He is more likely on the whole
to paint a slum in Soho than St. Paul's, and more likely
to do a lodging-house interior than a room at Hampton
Court. He may, of course, do either, but his necessary
detachment comes more easily in one case than the
other. The artist is, I believe, a very good critic if you
can make him drop his own job for a minute, and
really attend to some one else's work of art; but do

not go to him when he is on duty as an artist if you
want a sound judgment about objects of art. The
different visions I have discussed are like the different
gears of a motor-car, only that we sometimes step from
one gear into another without knowing it, and the
artist may be on the wrong gear for answering us truly.
Mr. Walter Sickert is likely to have a Sickert in his
eye when he gives us a panegyric on a bedroom candle-
stick.

ART AND SOCIALISM[1]

I AM not a Socialist, as I understand that word, nor
can I pretend to have worked out those complex esti-
mates of economic possibility which are needed before
one can endorse the hopeful forecasts of Lady Warwick,
Mr. Money, and Mr. Wells. What I propose to do here
is first to discuss what effect plutocracy, such as it is
to-day, has had of late, and is likely to have in the near
future, upon one of the things which I should like to
imagine continuing upon our planet—namely, art.
And then briefly to prognosticate its chances under
such a regime as my colleagues have sketched.

As I understand it, art is one of the chief organs of
what, for want of a better word, I must call the spiritual
life. It both stimulates and controls those indefinable
overtones of the material life of man which all of us
at moments feel to have a quality of permanence and
reality that does not belong to the rest of our experience.
Nature demands with no uncertain voice that the physical
needs of the body shall be satisfied first; but we feel
that our real human life only begins at the point where
that is accomplished, that the man who works at some
uncreative and uncongenial toil merely to earn enough

[1] Reprinted with considerable alterations from "The Great
State." (Harper. 1912.)

food to enable him to continue to work has not, properly speaking, a human life at all.

It is the argument of commercialism, as it once was of aristocracy, that the accumulation of surplus wealth in a few hands enables this spiritual life to maintain its existence, that no really valuable or useless work (for from this point of view only useless work has value) could exist in the community without such accumulations of wealth. The argument has been employed for the distinterested work of scientific research. A doctor of naturally liberal and generous impulses told me that he was becoming a reactionary simply because he feared that public bodies would never give the money necessary for research with anything like the same generosity as is now shown by the great plutocrats. But Sir Ray Lankester does not find that generosity sufficient, and is prepared at least to consider whether the State would not be more open-handed.

The situation as regards art and as regards the disinterested love of truth is so similar that we might expect this argument in favour of a plutocratic social order to hold equally well for both art and science, and that the artist would be a fervent upholder of the present system. As a matter of fact, the more representative artists have rarely been such, and not a few, though working their life long for the plutocracy, have been vehement Socialists.

Despairing of the conditions due to modern commercialism, it is not unnatural that lovers of beauty should look back with nostalgia to the age when society was controlled by a landed aristocracy. I believe, however, that from the point of view of the encouragement of great creative art there is not much difference between an aristocracy and a plutocracy. The aristocrat usually had taste, the plutocrat frequently has not. Now taste is of two kinds, the first consisting in the negative avoidance of all that is ill-considered and discordant,

the other positive and a by-product; it is that harmony
which always results from the expression of intense and
disinterested emotion. The aristocrat, by means of his
good taste of the negative kind, was able to come to
terms with the artist; the plutocrat was not. But both
alike desire to buy something which is incommensurate
with money. Both want art to be a background to their
radiant self-consciousness. They want to buy beauty
as they want to buy love; and the painter, picture-
dealer, and the pander try perennially to persuade them
that it is possible. But living beauty cannot be bought;
it must be won. I have said that the aristocrat, by his
taste, by his feeling for the accidentals of beauty, did
manage to get on to some kind of terms with the artist.
Hence the art of the eighteenth century, an art that is
prone before the distinguished patron, subtly and
deliciously flattering and yet always fine. In contrast
to that the art of the nineteenth century is coarse,
turbulent, clumsy. It marks the beginning of a revolt.
The artist just managed to let himself be coaxed and
cajoled by the aristocrat, but when the aristocratic was
succeeded by the plutocratic patron with less conciliatory
manners and no taste, the artist rebelled; and the
history of art in the nineteenth century is the history
of a band of heroic Ishmaelites, with no secure place
in the social system, with nothing to support them in the
unequal struggle but a dim sense of a new idea, the idea
of the freedom of art from all trammels and tyrannics.

The place that the artists left vacant at the plutocrat's
table had to be filled, and it was filled by a race new
in the history of the world, a race for whom no name
has yet been found, a race of psuedo-artists. As the
prostitute professes to sell love, so these gentlemen
professed to sell beauty, and they and their patrons
rollicked good-humouredly through the Victorian era.
They adopted the name and something of the manner
of artists; they intercepted not only the money, but

the titles and fame and glory which were intended for those whom they had supplanted. But, while they were yet feasting, there came an event which seemed at the time of no importance, but which was destined to change ultimately the face of things—the exhibition of ancient art at Manchester in 1857. And with this came Ruskin's address on the Political Economy of Art, a work which surprises by its prophetic foresight when we read it half a century later. These two things were the Mene Tekel of the orgy of Victorian Philistinism. The plutocrat saw through the deception; it was not beauty the pseudo-artist sold him, any more than it was love which the prostitute gave. He turned from it in disgust and decided that the only beauty he could buy was the dead beauty of the past. Thereupon set in the worship of *patine* and the age of forgery and the detection of forgery. I once remarked to a rich man that a statue by Rodin might be worthy even of his collection. He replied, "Show me a Rodin with the *patine* of the fifteenth century, and I will buy it."

Patine, then, the adventitious material beauty which age alone can give, has come to be the object of a reverence greater than that devoted to the idea which is enshrined within the work of art. People are right to admire *patine*. Nothing is more beautiful than gilded bronze of which time has taken toll until it is nothing but a faded shimmering splendour over depths of inscrutable gloom; nothing finer than the dull glow which Pentelic marble has gathered from past centuries of sunlight and warm Mediterranean breezes. *Patine* is good, but it is a surface charm added to the essential beauty of expression; its beauty is literally skin-deep. It can never come into being or exist in or for itself; no *patine* can make a bad work good, or the forgers would be justified. It is an adjectival and ancillary beauty scarcely worthy of our prolonged contemplation.

There is to the philosopher something pathetic in

the Plutocrat's worship of *patine*. It is, as it were, a compensation for his own want of it. On himself all the rough thumb and chisel marks of his maker—and he is self-made—stand as yet unpolished and raw; but his furniture, at least, shall have the distinction of age-long acquaintance with good manners.

But the net result of all this is that the artist has nothing to hope from the plutocrat. To him we must be grateful indeed for that brusque disillusionment of the real artist, the real artist who might have rubbed along uneasily for yet another century with his pre-decessor, the aristocrat. Let us be grateful to him for this; but we need not look to him for further benefits, and if we decide to keep him the artist must be content to be paid after he is dead and vicariously in the person of an art-dealer. The artist must be content to look on while sums are given for dead beauty, the tenth part of which, properly directed, would irrigate whole nations and stimulate once more the production of vital artistic expression.

I would not wish to appear to blame the plutocrat. He has often honestly done his best for art; the trouble is not of his making more than of the artist's, and the misunderstanding between art and commerce is bound to be complete. The artist, however mean and avaricious he may appear, knows that he cannot really sell himself for money any more than the philosopher or the scientific investigator can sell himself for money. He takes money in the hope that he may secure the opportunity for the free functioning of his creative power. If the patron could give him that instead of money he would bless him; but he cannot, and so he tries to get him to work not quite freely for money; and in revenge the artist indulges in all manner of insolences, even perhaps in sharp practices, which make the patron feel, with some justification, that he is the victim of ingratitude and wanton caprice. It is impossible that the artist should work for the plutocrat; he must work for himself, because it is only by so doing that he can perform the function for which he exists; it is only by working for himself that he can work for mankind.

If, then, the particular kind of accumulation of surplus wealth which we call plutocracy has failed, as surely it has signally failed, to stimulate the creative power of the imagination, what disposition of wealth might be conceived that would succeed better? First of all, a greater distribution of wealth, with a lower standard of ostentation, would, I think, do a great deal to improve things without any great change in other conditions. It is not enough known that the patronage which really counts to-day is exercised by quite small and humble people. These people with a few hundreds a year exercise a genuine patronage by buying pictures at ten, twenty, or occasionally thirty pounds, with real insight and understanding, thereby enabling the young Ishmaelite to live and function from the age of twenty to thirty or so, when perhaps he becomes known to richer buyers, those experienced spenders of money who are always more cautious, more anxious to buy an investment than a picture. These poor, intelligent first patrons to whom I allude belong mainly to the professional classes; they have none of the pretensions of the plutocrat and none of his ambitions. The work of art is not for them, as for him a decorative backcloth to his stage, but an idol and an inspiration. Merely to increase the number and potency of these people would already accomplish much; and this is to be noticed, that if wealth were more evenly distributed, if no one had a great deal of wealth, those who really cared for art would become the sole patrons, since for all it would be an appreciable sacrifice, and for none an impossibility. The man who only buys pictures when he has as many motor-cars as he can conceivably want would drop out as a patron altogether.

But even this would only foster the minor and private arts; and what the history of art definitely elucidates is that the greatest art has always been communal, the expression—in highly individualised ways, no doubt—of common aspirations and ideals.

Let us suppose, then, that society were so arranged that considerable surplus wealth lay in the hands of public bodies, both national and local; can we have any reasonable hope that they would show more skill in carrying out the delicate task of stimulating and using the creative power of the artist?

The immediate prospect is certainly not encouraging. Nothing, for instance, is more deplorable than to watch the patronage of our provincial museums. The gentlemen who administer these public funds naturally have not realised so acutely as private buyers the lesson so admirably taught at Christie's, that pseudo or Royal-Academic art is a bad investment. Nor is it better if we turn to national patronage. In Great Britain, at least, we cannot get a postage stamp or a penny even respectably designed, much less a public monument. Indeed, the tradition that all public British art shall be crassly mediocre and inexpressive is so firmly rooted that it seems to have almost the prestige of constitutional precedent.[1] Nor will any one who has watched a committee commissioning a presentation portrait, or even buying an old master, be in danger of taking too optimistic a view. With rare and shining exceptions, committees seem to be at the mercy of the lowest common denominator of their individual natures, which is dominated by fear of criticism; and fear and its attendant, compromise, are bad masters of the arts.

Speaking recently at Liverpool, Mr. Bernard Shaw placed the present situation as regards public art in its

---

[1] A precedent fully maintained by the war-monuments which have covered the English country-side since the above article was written.

true light. He declared that the corruption of taste and the emotional insincerity of the mass of the people had gone so far that any picture which pleased more than ten per cent. of the population should be immediately burned. . . .

This, then, is the fundamental fact we have to face. And it is this that gives us pause when we try to construct any conceivable system of public patronage.

For the modern artist puts the question of any socialistic—or, indeed, of any completely ordered—state, in its acutest form. He demands as an essential to the proper use of his powers a freedom from restraint such as no other workman expects. He must work when he feels inclined; he cannot work to order. Hence his frequent quarrels with the burgher who knows he has to work when he is disinclined, and cannot conceive why the artist should not do likewise. The burgher watches the artist's wayward and apparently quite unmethodical activity, and envies his job. Now, in any Socialistic State, if certain men are licensed to pursue the artistic calling, they are likely to be regarded by the other workers with some envy. There may be a competition for such soft jobs among those who are naturally work-shy, since it will be evident that the artist is not called to account in the same way as other workers.

If we suppose, as. seems not unlikely, in view of the immense numbers who become artists in our present social state, that there would be this competition for the artistic work of the community, what methods would be devised to select those required to fill the coveted posts ? Frankly, the history of art in the nineteenth century makes us shudder at the results that would follow. One scarcely knows whether they would be worse if Bumble or the Academy were judge. We only know that under any such conditions *none* of the artists whose work has ultimately counted in the spiritual development of the race would have been allowed to practise the coveted profession.

There is in truth, as Ruskin pointed out in his "Political Economy of Art," a gross and wanton waste under the present system. We have thousands of artists who are only so by accident and by name, on the one hand, and certainly many—one cannot tell how many— who have the special gift but have never had the peculiar opportunities which are to-day necessary to allow it to expand and function. But there is, what in an odd way consoles us, a blind chance that the gift and the opportunity may coincide; that Shelley and Browning may have a competence, and Cézanne a farm-house he could retire to. Bureaucratic Socialism would, it seems take away even this blind chance that mankind may benefit by its least appreciable, most elusive treasures, and would carefully organise the complete suppression of original creative power; would organise into a universal and all-embracing tyranny the already overweening and disastrous power of endowed official art. For we must face the fact that the average man has two qualities which would make the proper selection of the artist almost impossible. He has, first of all, a touching proclivity to awe-struck admiration of whatever is presented to him as noble by a constituted authority; and, secondly, a complete absence of any immediate reaction to a work of art until his judgment has thus been hypnotised by the voice of authority. Then, and not till then, he sees, or swears he sees, those adorable Emperor's clothes that he is always agape for.

I am speaking, of course, of present conditions, of a populace whose emotional life has been drugged by the sugared poison of pseudo-art, a populace saturated with snobbishness, and regarding art chiefly for its value as a symbol of social distinctions. There have been times when such a system of public patronage as we are discussing might not have been altogether disastrous. Times when the guilds represented more or less adequately the genuine artistic intelligence of the time; but the creation, first of all, of aristocratic art, and finally of pseudo-art, have brought it about that almost any officially organised system would at the present moment stereotype all the worst features of modern art.

Now, in thus putting forward the extreme difficulties of any system of publicly controlled art, we are emphasising perhaps too much the idea of the artist as a creator of purely ideal and abstract works, as the medium of inspiration and the source of revelation. It is the artist as prophet and priest that we have been considering, the artist who is the articulate soul of mankind. Now, in the present commercial State, at a time when such handiwork as is not admirably fitted to some purely utilitarian purpose has become inanely fatuous and grotesque, the artist in this sense has undoubtedly become of supreme importance as a protestant, as one who proclaims that art is a reasonable function, and one that proceeds by a nice adjustment of means to ends. But if we suppose a state in which all the ordinary objects of daily life—our chairs and tables, our carpets and pottery—expressed something of this reasonableness instead of a crazy and vapid fantasy the artist as a pure creator might become, not indeed of less import-ance—rather more—but a less acute necessity to our general living than he is to-day. Something of the sanity and purposefulness of his attitude might con-ceivably become infused into the work of the ordinary craftsman, something, too, of his creative energy and delight in work. We must, therefore, turn for a moment from the abstractly creative artist to the applied arts and those who practise them.

We are so far obliged to protect ourselves from the implications of modern life that without a special effort it is hard to conceive the enormous quantity of "art" that is annually produced and consumed. For the special purpose of realising it I take the pains to write the succeeding paragraphs in a railway refreshment-room, where I am actually looking at those terribly familiar but fortunately fleeting images which such places afford. And one must remember that public places of this kind merely reflect the average citizen's soul, as expressed in his home.

The space my eye travels over is a small one, but I am appalled at the amount of "art" that it harbours. The window towards which I look is filled in its lower part by stained glass; within a highly elaborate border, designed by some one who knew the conventions of thirteenth-century glass, is a pattern of yellow and purple vine leaves with bunches of grapes, and flitting about among these many small birds. In front is a lace curtain with patterns taken from at least four centuries and as many countries. On the walls, up to a height of four feet, is a covering of lincrusta walton stamped with a complicated pattern in two colours, with sham silver medallions. Above that a moulding but an inch wide, and yet creeping throughout its whole with a degenerate descendant of a Græco-Roman carved guilloche pattern; this has evidently been cut out of the wood by machine or stamped out of some composition—its nature is so perfectly concealed that it is hard to say which. Above this is a wall-paper in which an effect of eighteenth-century satin brocade is imitated by shaded staining of the paper. Each of the little refreshment-tables has two cloths, one arranged symmetrically with the table, the other a highly ornate printed cotton arranged "artistically" in a diagonal position. In the centre of each table is a large pot in which every beautiful quality in the material and making of pots has been carefully obliterated by methods each of which implies profound scientific knowledge and great inventive talent. Within each pot is a plant with large dark green leaves, apparently made of india-rubber. This painful catalogue makes up only a small part of the inventory of the "art" of the restaurant. If I were to go on to tell of the legs of the tables, of the electric-light fittings, of the chairs into the wooden seats of which some tremendous mechanical force has deeply impressed a large distorted anthemion—if I were to tell of all these things, my reader and I might both begin to realise with painful acuteness something of the horrible toil involved in all this display. Display is indeed the end and explanation of it all. Not one of these things has been made because the maker enjoyed the making; not one has been bought because its contemplation would give any one any pleasure, but solely because each of these things is accepted as a symbol of a particular social status. I say their contemplation can give no one pleasure; they are there because their absence would be resented by the average man who regards a large amount of futile display as in some way inseparable from the conditions of that well-to-do life to which he belongs or aspires to belong. If everything were merely clean and serviceable he would proclaim the place bare and uncomfortable.

The doctor who lines his waiting-room with bad photogravures and worse etchings is acting on exactly the same principle; in short, nearly all our "art" is made, bought, and sold merely for its value as an indication of social status.

Now consider the case of those men whose life-work it is to stimulate this eczematous eruption of pattern on the surface of modern manufactures. They are by far the most numerous "artists" in the country. Each of them has not only learned to draw, but has learned by sheer application to put forms together with a similitude of that coherence which creative impulse gives. Probably each of them has somewhere within him something of that creative impulse which is the inspiration and

delight of every savage and primitive craftsman; but
in these manufacturer's designers the pressure of commercial life has crushed and atrophied that creative
impulse completely. Their business is to produce, not
expressive design, but dead patterns. They are compelled, therefore, to spend their lives behaving in an
entirely idiotic and senseless manner, and that with
the certainty that no one will ever get positive pleasure
from the result; for one may hazard the statement
that until I made the effort just now, no one of the
thousands who use the refreshment-rooms ever really
looked at the designs.

This question of the creation and consumption of
art tends to become more and more pressing. I have
shown just now what an immense mass of art is consumed, but this is not the same art as that which the
genuine artist produces. The work of the truly creative
artist is not merely useless to the social man—it appears
to be noxious and inassimilable. Before art can be
"consumed" the artistic idea must undergo a process of
disinfection. It must have had extracted and removed
from it all, or nearly all, that makes it æsthetically
valuable. What occurs when a great artist creates a
new idea is somewhat as follows: We know the process
well enough, since an example of it has occurred within
the last fifty years. An artist attains to a new vision.
He grasps this with such conviction that he is able to
express it in his work. Those few people in his immediate surroundings who have the faculty of æsthetic
perception become very much excited by the new
vision. The average man, on the other hand, lacks this
faculty and, moreover, instinctively protects the rounded
perfection of his universe of thought and feeling from
the intrusion of new experience; in consequence he
becomes extremely irritated by the sight of works which
appear to him completely unintelligible. The misunderstanding between this small minority and the

public becomes violent. Then some of the more intelligent writers on art recognise that the new idea is really related to past æsthetic expressions which have become recognised. Then a clever artist, without any individual vision of his own, sees the possibility of using a modification of the new idea, and makes an ingenious compromise between it and the old, generally accepted notions of art. The public, which has been irritated by its incomprehension of the new idea, finding the compromise just intelligible, and delighted to find itself cleverer than it thought, acclaims the compromising intermediary as a genius. The process of disinfection thus begun goes on with increasing energy and rapidity, and before long the travesty of the new idea is completely assimilable by the social organism. The public, after swallowing innumerable imitations of the new idea, may even at last reluctantly accept the original creator as a great man, but generally not until he has been dead for some time and has become a vague and mythical figure.

It is literally true to say that the imitations of works of art are more assimilable by the public than originals, and therefore always tend to fetch a higher price in the market at the moment of their production.

The fact is that the average man uses art entirely for its symbolic value. Art is in fact the symbolic currency of the world. The possession of rare and much-coveted works of art is regarded as a sign of national greatness. The growth and development of the Kaiser Friedrich Museum was due to the active support of the Emperor William II., a man whose distaste for genuine art is notorious, but whose sense of the symbolic was highly developed. Large and expensively ornamented buildings become symbols of municipal greatness. The amount of useless ornaments on the façades of their offices is a valuable symbol of the financial exuberance of big commercial undertakings;

c

and, finally, the social status of the individual is expressed to the admiring or envious outer world by the streamlines of an aristocratic motor-car, or the superfluity of lace curtains in the front windows of a genteel suburban villa.

The social man, then, lives in a world of symbols, and though he presses other things into his service, such, for instance, as kings, footmen, dogs, women, he finds in art his richest reservoir of symbolic currency. But in a world of symbolists the creative artist and the creative man of science appear in strange isolation as the only people who are not symbolists. They alone are up against certain relations which do not stand for something else, but appear to have ultimate value, to be real.

Art as a symbolic currency is an important means of the instinctive life of man, but art as created by the artist is in violent revolt against the instinctive life, since it is an expression of the reflective and fully conscious life. It is natural enough, then, that before it can be used by the instinctive life it must be deprived by travesty of its too violent assertion of its own reality. Travesty is necessary at first to make it assimilable, but in the end long familiarity may rob even original works of art of their insistence, so that, finally, even the great masterpieces may become the most cherished symbols of the lords of the instinctive life—may, as in fact they frequently do, become the property of millionaires.

A great deal of misunderstanding and ill-feeling between the artist and the public comes from a failure to realise the necessity of this process of assimilation of the work of art to the needs of the instinctive life.

I suspect that a very similar process takes place with regard to truth. In order that truth may not outrage too violently the passions and egoisms of the instinctive life, it too must undergo a process of deformation.

Society, for example, accepts as much of the ascertainable truth as it can stand at a given period in the form of the doctrine of its organised religion.

Now what effect would the development of the Great State which this book anticipates have upon all this? First, I suppose that the fact that every one had to work might produce a new reverence, especially in the governing body, for work, a new sense of disgust and horror at wasteful and purposeless work. Mr. Money has written of waste of work; here in unwanted pseudo-art is another colossal waste. Add to this ideal of economy in work the presumption that the workers in every craft would be more throughly organised and would have a more decisive voice in the nature and quality of their productions. Under the present system of commercialism the one object, and the complete justification, of producing any article is, that it can be made either by its intrinsic value, or by the fictitious value put upon it by advertisement, to sell with a sufficient profit to the manufacturer. In any socialistic state, I imagine—and to a large extent the Great State will be socialistic at least—there would not be this same automatic justification for manufacture; people would not be induced artificially to buy what they did not want, and in this way a more genuine scale of values would be developed. Moreover, the workman would be in a better position to say how things should be made. After years of a purely commercial standard, there is left even now, in the average workman, a certain bias in favour of sound and reasonable workmanship as opposed to the ingenious manufacture of fatuous and fraudulent objects; and, if we suppose the immediate pressure of sheer necessity to be removed, it is probable that the craftsman, acting through his guild organisations, would determine to some extent the methods of manufacture. Guilds might, indeed, regain something of the political influence that gave us the Gothic cathedrals of the Middle Ages. It is quite probable that this guild influence would act as a check on some innovations in manufacture which, though bringing in a profit, are really disastrous to the community at large. Of such a nature are all the so-called improvements whereby decoration, the whole value of which consists in its expressive power, is multiplied indefinitely by machinery. When once the question of the desirability of any and every production came to be discussed, as it would be in the Great State, it would inevitably follow that some reasonable and scientific classifications would be undertaken with regard to machinery. That is to say, it would be considered in what processes and to what degree machinery ought to replace handiwork, both from the point of view of the community as a whole and from that of the producer. So far as I know, this has never been undertaken even with regard to mere economy, no one having calculated with precision how far the longer life of certain hand-made articles does not more than compensate for increased cost of production. And I suppose that in the Great State other things besides mere economy would come into the calculation. The Great State will live, not hoard.

It is probable that in many directions we should extend mechanical operations immensely, that such things as the actual construction of buildings, the mere laying and placing of the walls might become increasingly mechanical. Such methods, if confined to purely structural elements, are capable of beauty of a special kind, since they can express the ordered ideas of proportion, balance, and interval as conceived by the creative mind of the architect. But in process of time one might hope to see a sharp line of division between work of this kind and such purely expressive and non-utilitarian design as we call ornament; and it would be felt clearly that into this field no mechanical device should intrude, that, while ornament might be dispensed with, it could never be imitated, since its only reason for being is that it conveys the vital expressive power of a human mind acting constantly and directly upon matter.

Finally, I suppose that in the Great State we might hope to see such a considerable levelling of social conditions that the false values put upon art by its symbolising of social status would be largely destroyed, and, the pressure of mere opinion being relieved, people would develop some more immediate reaction to the work of art than they can at present achieve.

Supposing, then, that under the Great State it was found impossible, at all events at first, to stimulate and organise the abstract creative power of the pure artist, the balance might after all be in favour of the new order if the whole practice of applied art could once more become rational and purposeful. In a world where the objects of daily use and ornament were made with practical common sense, the æsthetic sense would need far less to seek consolation and repose in works of pure art.

Nevertheless, in the long run mankind will not allow this function, which is necessary to its spiritual life, to lapse entirely. I imagine, however, that it would be much safer to penalise rather than to stimulate such activity, and that simply in order to sift out those with a genuine passion from those who are merely attracted by the apparent ease of the pursuit. I imagine that the artist would naturally turn to one of the applied arts as his means of livelihood; and we should get the artist coming out of the *bottéga*, as he did in fifteenth-century Florence. There are, moreover, innumerable crafts, even besides those that are definitely artistic, which, if pursued for short hours—Sir Leo Money has shown how short these hours might be—would leave a man free to pursue other callings in his leisure.

The majority of poets to-day are artists in this position. It is comparatively rare for any one to make of poetry his actual means of livelihood. Our poets are, first of all, clerks, critics, civil servants, or postmen. I very much doubt if it would be a serious loss to the community if the pure graphic artist were in the same position. That is to say, that all our pictures would be made by amateurs. It is quite possible to suppose that this would be not a loss, but a great gain. The painter's means of livelihood would probably be some craft in which his artistic powers would be constantly occupied, though at a lower tension and in a humbler way. The Great State aims at human freedom; essentially, it is an organisation for leisure—out of which art grows; it is only a purely bureaucratic Socialism that would attempt to control the æsthetic lives of men.

So I conceive that those in whom the instinct for abstract creative art was strongest would find ample opportunities for its exercise, and that the temptation to stimulate this particular activity would be easily resisted by those who had no powerful inner compulsion.

In the Great State, moreover, and in any sane Socialism, there would be opportunity for a large amount of purely private buying and selling. Mr. Wells's Modern Utopia, for example, hypothecates a vast superstructure of private trading. A painter might sell his pictures to those who were engaged in more lucrative employment, though one supposes that with the much more equal distribution of wealth the sums available for this would be incomparably smaller than at present; a picture would not be a speculation, but a pleasure, and no one would become an artist in the hope of making a fortune.

Ultimately, of course, when art had been purified of its present unreality by a prolonged contact with the crafts, society would gain a new confidence in its collective artistic judgment, and might even boldly assume the responsibility which at present it knows it is unable to face. It might choose its poets and painters and philosophers and deep investigators, and make of such men and women a new kind of kings.

ART AND SCIENCE[1]

THE author of an illuminating article, "The Place of Science," in *The Athenæum* for April 11th, distinguishes between two aspects of intellectual activity in scientific work. Of these two aspects one derives its motive power from curiosity, and this deals with particular facts. It is only when, through curiosity, man has accumulated a mass of particular observations that the second intellectual activity manifests itself, and in this the motive is the satisfaction which the mind gets from the contemplation of inevitable relations. To secure this end the utmost possible generalisation is necessary.

In a later article S. says boldly that this satisfaction is an æsthetic satisfaction: "It is in its æsthetic value that the justification of the scientific theory is to be found, and with it the justification of the scientific method." I should like to pose to S. at this point the question of whether a theory that disregarded facts would have equal value for science with one which agreed with facts. I suppose he would say No; and yet, so far as I can see, there would be no purely æsthetic reason why it should not. The æsthetic value of a theory would surely depend solely on the perfection and complexity of the unity attained, and I imagine that many systems of scholastic theology, and even some more recent systems of metaphysics, have only this æsthetic value. I suspect that the æsthetic value of a theory is not really sufficient to justify the intellectual effort entailed unless, as in a true scientific theory—by which I mean

[1] Athenæum, 1919.

a theory which embraces all the known relevant facts—the æsthetic value is reinforced by the curiosity value which comes in when we believe it to be true. But now, returning to art, let me try to describe rather more clearly its analogies with science.

Both of these aspects—the particularising and the generalising—have their counterparts in art. Curiosity impels the artist to the consideration of every possible form in nature: under its stimulus he tends to accept each form in all its particularity as a given, unalterable fact. The other kind of intellectual activity impels the artist to attempt the reduction of all forms, as it were, to some common denominator which will make them comparable with one another. It impels him to discover some æsthetically intelligible principle in various forms, and even to envisage the possibility of some kind of abstract form in the æsthetic contemplation of which the mind would attain satisfaction—a satisfaction curiously parallel to that which the mind gets from the intellectual recognition of abstract truth.

If we consider the effects of these two kinds of intellectual activity, or rather their exact analogues, in art, we have to note that in so far as the artist's curiosity remains a purely intellectual curiosity it interferes with the perfection and purity of the work of art by introducing an alien and non-æsthetic element and appealing to non-æsthetic desires; in so far as it merely supplies the artist with new motives and a richer material out of which to build his designs, it is useful but subsidiary. Thus the objection to a "subject picture," in so far as one remains conscious of the subject as something outside of, and apart from, the form, is a valid objection to the intrusion of intellect, of however rudimentary a kind, into an æsthetic whole. The ordinary historical pictures of our annual shows will furnish perfect examples of such an intrusion, since they exhibit innumerable appeals to intellectual recognitions without which the pictures would be meaningless. Without some previous knowledge of Caligula or Mary Queen of Scots we are likely to miss our way in a great deal of what passes for art to-day.

The case of the generalising intellect, or rather its analogue, in art is more difficult. Here the recognition of relations is immediate and sensational—perhaps we ought to consider it as curiously akin to those cases of mathematical geniuses who have immediate intuition of mathematical relations which it is beyond their powers to prove—so that it is by analogy that we may talk of it at all as intellectual. But the analogy is so close that I hope it may justify the use I here suggest. For in both cases the utmost possible generalisation is aimed at, and in both the mind is held in delighted equilibrium by the contemplation of the inevitable relations of all the parts in the whole, so that no need exists to make reference to what is outside the unity, and this becomes for the time being a universe.

It will be seen how close the analogies are between the methods and aims of art and science, and yet there remains an obstinate doubt in the mind whether at any point they are identical. Probably in order to get much further we must wait for the psychologists to solve a number of problems; meanwhile this at least must be pointed out—that, allowing that the motives of science are emotional, many of its processes are purely intellectual, that is to say, mechanical. They could be performed by a perfectly non-sentient, emotionless brain, whereas at no point in the process of art can we drop feeling. There is something in the common phraseology by which we talk of *seeing* a point or an argument, whereas we *feel* the harmony of a work of art; and for some reason we attach a more constant emotional quality to feeling than to seeing, which is in more frequent request for coldly practical ends.

From the merest rudiments of pure sensation up to

the highest efforts of design each point in the process
of art is inevitably accompanied by pleasure; it cannot
proceed without it. If we describe the process of art
as a logic of sensation, we must remember that the
premises are sensations, and that the conclusion can
only be drawn from them by one who is in an emotional
state with regard to them. Thus a harmony in music
cannot be perceived by a person who merely hears
accurately the notes which compose it—it can only be
recognised when the relations of those notes to one
another are accompanied by emotion. It is quite true
that the recognition of inevitability in thought is nor-
mally accompanied by a pleasurable emotion, and that
the desire for this mental pleasure is the motive force
which impels to the making of scientific theory. But
the inevitability of the relations remains equally definite
and demonstrable whether the emotion accompanies
it or not, whereas an æsthetic harmony simply does
not exist without the emotional state. The harmony
is not *true*—to use our analogy—unless it is felt with
emotion.

None the less, perhaps, the highest pleasure in art
is identical with the highest pleasure in scientific theory.
The emotion which accompanies the clear recognition
of unity in a complex seems to be so similar in art and
in science that it is difficult not to suppose that they
are psychologically the same. It is, as it were, the final
stage of both processes. This unity-emotion in science
supervenes upon a process of pure mechanical reasoning;
in art it supervenes upon a process of which emotion
has all along been an essential concomitant.

It may be that in the complete apprehension of a
work of art there occurs more than one kind of feeling.
There is generally a basis of purely physiological pleasure,
as in seeing pure colours or hearing pure sounds;
then there is the specifically æsthetic emotion by means
of which the necessity of relations is apprehended, and

which corresponds in science to the purely logical process; and finally there is the unity-emotion, which may not improbably be of an identical kind in both art and science.

In the art of painting we may distinguish between the unity of texture and the unity of design. I know quite well that these are not really completely separable, and that they are to some extent mutually dependent; but they may be regarded as separate for the purpose of focussing our attention. Certainly we can think of pictures in which the general architecture of the design is in no way striking or remarkable which yet please us by the perfection of the texture, that is to say, the ease with which we apprehend the necessary relationship of one shape, tone or colour with its immediately surrounding shapes, tones or colours; our æsthetic sense is continually aroused and satisfied by the succession of inevitable relationships. On the other hand, we know of works of art in which the unity and complexity of the texture strike us far less than the inevitable and significant relationship of the main divisions of the design—pictures in which we should say that the composition was the most striking beauty. It is when the composition of a picture, adequately supported as it must be by significance of texture, reveals to us the most surprising and yet inevitable relationships that we get most strongly the final unity-emotion of a work of art. It is these pictures that are, as S. would say of certain theories, the most significant for contemplation. Nor before such works can we help implicitly attributing to their authors the same kind of power which in science we should call "great intellect," though perhaps in both the term "great imaginative organisation" would be better.

THE ART OF THE BUSHMEN [1]

In the history of mankind drawing has at different times and among different races expressed so many different conceptions, and has used such various means, that it would seem to be not one art, but many. It would seem, indeed, that it has its origins in several quite distinct instincts of the human race, and it may not be altogether unimportant even for the modern draughtsman to investigate these instincts in their simpler manifestations in order to check and control his own methods. The primitive drawing of our own race is singularly like that of children. Its most striking peculiarity is the extent to which it is dominated by the concepts of language. In a child's drawing we find a number of forms which have scarcely any reference to actual appearances, but which directly symbolise the most significant concepts of the thing represented. For a child, a man is the sum of the concept's head (which in turn consists of eyes, nose, mouth), of his arms, his hands (five fingers), his legs and his feet. Torso is not a concept which interests him, and it is, therefore, usually reduced to a single line which serves to link the concept-symbol head with those of the legs. The child does, of course, know that the figure thus drawn is not like a man, but it is a kind of hieroglyphic script for a man, and satisfies his desire for expression. Precisely the same phenomenon occurs in primitive art; the symbols for concepts gradually take on more and more of the likeness to appearances, but the mode of approach remains even in comparatively advanced periods the same. The artist does not seek to transfer a visual sensation to paper, but to express

[1] Burlington Magazine, 1910.

a mental image which is coloured by his conceptual habits.

Prof. Loewy[1] has investigated the laws which govern representation in early art, and has shown that the influence of the early artist's ideas of conceptual symbolism persist in Greek sculpture down to the time of Lysippus. He enumerates seven peculiarities of early drawing, of which the most important are that the figures are shown with each of their parts in its broadest aspect, and that the forms are stylised—*i.e.*, present linear formations that are regular or tend to regularity.

Of the first of these peculiarities Egyptian and Assyrian sculpture, even of the latest and most developed periods, afford constant examples. We see there the head in profile, the eye full face, the shoulders and breast full face, and by a sudden twist in the body the legs and feet again in profile. In this way each part is presented in that aspect which most clearly expresses its corresponding visual concepts. Thus a foot is much more clearly denoted by its profile view than by the rendering of its frontal appearance—while no one who was asked to think of an eye would visualise it to himself in any other than a full-face view. In such art, then, the body is twisted about so that each part may be represented by that aspect which the mental image aroused by the name of the part would have, and the figure becomes an ingenious compound of typical conceptual images. In the case of the head two aspects are accepted as symbolic of the concept "head," the profile and the full-face; but it is very late in the development of art before men are willing to accept any intermediate position as intelligible or satisfactory. It is generally supposed that early art avoids foreshortening because of its difficulty. One may suppose rather that it is because the foreshortened view of a member corres-

[1] "The Rendering of Nature in Early Greek Art." By Emmanuel Loewy. Translated by J. Fothergill. Duckworth. 1907.

ponds so ill with the normal conceptual image, and is therefore not accepted as sufficiently expressive of the idea. Yet another of the pecularities named by Prof. Loewy must be mentioned, namely, that the "conformation and movement of the figures and their parts are limited to a few typical shapes." And these movements are always of the simplest kinds, since they are governed by the necessity of displaying each member in its broadest and most explicit aspect. In particular the crossing of one limb over another is avoided as confusing.

Such, in brief outline, are some of the main principles of drawing both among primitive peoples and among our own children. It is not a little surprising then to find, when we turn to Miss Tongue's careful copies of the drawings executed by the Bushmen of South Africa,[1] that the principles are more often contradicted than exemplified. We find, it is true, a certain barbaric crudity and simplicity which give these drawings a superficial resemblance to children's drawings or those of primitive times, but a careful examination will show how different they are. The drawings are of different periods, though none of them probably are of any considerable antiquity, since the habit of painting over an artist's work when once he was forgotten obtained among the bushmen no less than with more civilised people. These drawings are also of very different degrees of skill. They represent for the most part scenes of the chase and war, dances and festivals, and in one case there is an illustration to a bushman story and one figure is supposed to represent a ghost. There is no evidence of deliberate decorative purpose in these paintings. The figures are cast upon the walls of the cave in such a way as to represent, roughly, the actual

---

[1] "Bushman Drawings," copied by M. Helen Tongue, with a preface by Henry Balfour. Oxford: Clarendon Press. 1909. £3 3s. net.

scenes.[1] Nothing could be more unlike primitive art
than some of these scenes. For instance, the battle
fought between two tribes over the possession of some
cattle, is entirely unlike battle scenes such as we find
in early Assyrian reliefs. There the battle is schematic,
all the soldiers of one side are in profile to right, all the
soldiers of the opposing side are in profile to left. The
whole scene is perfectly clear to the intelligence, it
follows the mental image of what a battle ought to
be, but is entirely unlike what a battle ever is. Now,
in the Bushman drawing there is nothing truly schematic;
it is difficult to find out the soldiers of the two sides;
they are all mixed up in a confused hurly-burly, some
charging, others flying, and here and there single combats
going on at a distance from the main battle. But more
than this, the men are in every conceivable attitude,
running, standing, kneeling, crouching, or turning
sharply round in the middle of flight to face the enemy
once more.

In fact we have, in all its confusion, all its indeter-
minate variety and accident, a rough silhouette of the
actual appearance of such a scene as viewed from
above, for the Bushman makes this sacrifice of actual
appearance to lucidity of statement—that he represents
the figures as spread out over the ground, and not as
seen one behind another.

Or take again Plate XI of Miss Tongue's album;
the scene is the Veldt with elands and rheboks scattered
over its surface. The animals are arranged in the most
natural and casual manner; sometimes in this case
part of one animal is hidden by the animal in front;

[1] This absence of decorative feeling may be due to the irregular
and vague outlines of the picture space. It is when the picture
must be fitted within determined limits that decoration begins.
I have noticed that children's drawings are never decorative when
they have the whole surface of a sheet of paper to draw on, but
they will design a frieze with well-marked rhythm when they have
only a narrow strip.

FIG. 1.

FIG. 2.

FIG. 3.

FIG. 4.

FIG. 5.

but what strikes one most is the fact that extremely complicated poses are rendered with the same ease as the more frequent profile view, and that momentary actions are treated with photographic verisimilitude. See Figs. 1 and 2.

Another surprising instance of this is shown in Fig. 3, taken from Plate XIX of Miss Tongue's book, and giving a rhebok seen from behind in a most difficult and complicated attitude. Or again, the man running in Fig. 5. Here is the silhouette of a most complicated gesture with foreshortening of one thigh and crossing of the arm holding the bow over the torso, rendered with apparent certainty and striking verisimilitude. Most curious of all are the cases of which Fig. 4 is an example, of animals trotting, in which the gesture is seen by us to be true only because our slow and imperfect vision has been helped out by the instantaneous photograph. Fifty years ago we should have rejected such a rendering as absurd; we now know it to be a correct statement of one movement in the action of trotting.

Another point to be noticed is that in primitive and in children's art such features as eyes, ears, horns, tails, since they correspond to well-marked concepts, always tend to be drawn disproportionately large and prominent. Now, in the Bushman drawings, the eye, the most significant of all, is frequently omitted, and when represented bears its true proportion to the head. Similarly, horns, ears and tails are never exaggerated. Indeed, however faulty these drawings may be, they have one great quality, namely, that each figure is seen as a single entity, and the general character of the silhouette is aimed at rather than a sum of the parts. Those who have taught drawing to children will know with what infinite pains civilised man arrives at this power.

By way of contrast to these extraordinary performances of the Bushman draughtsman, I give in outline

Fig. 6, the two horses of a chariot on an early—Dipylon
—Greek vase. The man who drew it was incomparably
more of an artist; but how entirely his intellectual and
conceptual way of handling phenomena has obscured
his vision! His two horses are a sum of concept-
symbols, arranged with great orderliness and with a
decorative feeling, but without any sort of likeness to
appearance. Mr. Balfour, in his preface to Miss Tongue's
book, notices briefly some of these striking characteristics of the Bushman drawings. He says:

"The paintings are remarkable not only for the
realism exhibited by so many, but also for a freedom

from the limitation to delineation in profile which
characterises for the most
part the drawings of primitive peoples, especially where
animals are concerned. Attitudes of a kind difficult to
render were ventured upon
without hesitation, and an
appreciation even of the
rudiments of perspective is
occasionally to be noted,

FIG. 6.

though only in a crude and uncertain form. The practice
of endeavouring to represent more than could be seen
at one time, a habit so characteristic of the art of primitive peoples as also of civilised children, is far less
noticeable in Bushman art than might have been expected from the rudimentary general culture of these
people, and one does not see instances of *both* eyes
being indicated upon a profile face, or a mouth in
profile on a full face, such as are so familiar in the
undeveloped art of children and of most backward
races."

Since, then, Bushman drawing has little analogy to
the primitive art of our own races, to what can we

relate it? The Bushmen of Australia have apparently something of the same power of transcribing pure visual images, but the most striking case is that of Palæolithic man. In the caves of the Dordogne and of Altamira in Spain, Palæolithic man has left paintings which date from about 10,000 B.C., in which, as far as mere naturalism of representation of animals goes, he has surpassed anything that not only our own primitive peoples, but even the most accomplished animal draughtsmen

Fig. 7.

have ever achieved. Fig. 7 shows in outline a bison from Altamira. The certainty and completeness of the pose, the perfect rhythm and the astonishing verisimilitude of the movement are evident even in this. The Altamira drawings show a much higher level of accomplishment than those of the Bushmen, but the general likeness is so great as to have suggested the idea that the Bushmen are descendants of Palæolithic man who have remained at the same rudimentary stage as regards the other arts of life, and have retained something of their unique power of visual transcription.

Whether this be so or not, it is to be noted that all

the peoples whose drawing shows this peculiar power of visualisation belong to what we call the lowest of savages; they are certainly the least civilisable, and the South African Bushmen are regarded by other native races in much the same way that we look upon negroes. It would seem not impossible that the very perfection of vision, and presumably of the other senses[1] with which the Bushmen and Palæolithic man were endowed, fitted them so perfectly to their surroundings that there was no necessity to develop the mechanical arts beyond the elementary instruments of the chase. We must suppose that Neolithic man, on the other hand, was less perfectly adapted to his surroundings, but that his sensual defects were more than compensated for by increased intellectual power. This greater intellectual power manifested itself in his desire to classify phenomena, and the conceptual view of nature began to predominate. And it was this habit of thinking of things in terms of concepts which deprived him for ages of the power to see what they looked like. With Neolithic man drawing came to express man's thought about things rather than his sensations of them, or rather, when he tried to reproduce his sensations, his habits of thought intervened, and dictated to his hand orderly, lucid, but entirely non-naturalistic forms.

How deeply these visual-conceptual habits of Neolithic man have sunk into our natures may be seen by their effects upon hysterical patients, a statement which I owe to the kindness of Dr. Henry Head, F.R.S. If the word "chest" is mentioned most people see a vague image of a flat surface on which are marked the sternum and the pectoral muscles; when the word "back" is given, they see another flat or almost flat surface with markings of the spine and the shoulder-blades; but scarcely any one, having these two mental images called

[1] This is certainly the case with the Australian Bushmen.

up, thinks of them as parts of a continuous cylindrical body. Now, in the case of some hysterical patients anæsthesia is found just over some part of the body which has been isolated from the rest in thought by means of the conceptual image. It will occur, for instance, in the chest, but will not go beyond the limits which the conceptualised visual image of a chest defines. Or it will be associated with the concept hand, and will stop short at the wrists. It is not surprising, then, that a mode of handling the continuum of natural appearance, which dictates even the behaviour of disease, should have profoundly modified all artistic representations of nature since the conceptual habit first became strongly marked in Neolithic man. An actual definition of drawing given by a child may be quoted in this connection, "First I think, and then I draw a line round my think."

It would be an exaggeration to suppose that Palæolithic and Bushman drawings are entirely uninfluenced by the concepts which even the most primitive people must form. Indeed, the preference for the profile view of animals—though as we have seen other aspects are frequent—would alone indicate this, but they appear to have been at a stage of intellectual development where the concepts were not so clearly grasped as to have begun to interfere with perception, and where therefore the retinal image passed into a clear memory picture with scarcely any intervening mental process. In the art of even civilised man we may, I think, find great variations in the extent to which the conceptualising of visual images has proceeded. Egyptian and Assyrian art remained intensely conceptual throughout, no serious attempt was made to give greater verisimilitude to the symbols employed. The Mycenæan artists, on the other hand, seem to have been appreciably more perceptual, but the Greeks returned to an intensely conceptualised symbolism in which some of their greatest works of art were expressed, and only very gradually did they modify their formulæ so as to admit of some approach to verisimilitude, and even so the appeal to vision was rather by way of correcting and revising accepted conceptual images than as the foundation of a work of art. The art of China, and still more of Japan, has been distinctly more perceptual. Indeed, the Japanese drawings of birds and animals approach

FIG. 8.

more nearly than those of any other civilised people to the immediacy and rapidity of transcription of Bushman and Palæolithic art. The Bushman silhouettes of cranes (Fig. 8) might almost have come from a Japanese screen. Like Japanese drawings, they show an alertness to accept the silhouette as a single whole instead of reconstructing it from separately apprehended parts. It is partly due to Japanese influence that our own Impressionists have made an attempt to get back to that ultra-primitive directness of vision. Indeed they deliberately sought to deconceptualise art. The artist of to-day has therefore to some extent a choice before him of whether he will *think* form like the early artists of European races or merely *see* it like the Bushmen. Whichever his choice, the study of these drawings can hardly fail to be of profound interest. The Bushmen paintings on the walls of caves and sheltered rocks are fast disappearing; the race itself, of which Miss Bleek gives a fascinating account, is now nothing but a remnant. The treatment that they have received at the hands of the white settlers does not seem to have been conspicuously more sympathetic or intelligent than that meted out to them by negro conquerors, and thus the opportunity of solving some of the most interesting problems of human development has been for ever lost. The gratitude of all students of art is due to Miss Tongue and Miss Bleek, by whose zeal and industry these remains of a most curious phase of primitive art have been adequately recorded.

NEGRO SCULPTURE[1]

WHAT a comfortable mental furniture the generalisations of a century ago must have afforded! What a right little, tight little, round little world it was when Greece was the only source of culture, when Greek art, even in Roman copies, was the only indisputable art, except for some Renaissance repetitions! Philosophy, the love of truth, liberty, architecture, poetry, drama, and for all we know music—all these were the fruits of a special kind of life, each assisted the development of the other, each was really dependent on all the rest. Consequently if we could only learn the

[1] Athenæum, 1920.

Greek lessons of political freedom and intellectual
self-consciousness all the rest would be added unto us.

And now, in the last sixty years, knowledge and
perception have poured upon us so fast that the whole
well-ordered system has been blown away, and we stand
bare to the blast, scarcely able to snatch a hasty generalisation or two to cover our nakedness for a moment.

Our desperate plight comes home to one at the
Chelsea Book Club, where are some thirty chosen
specimens of negro sculpture. If to our ancestors
the poor Indian had "an untutored mind," the Con-
golese's ignorance and savagery must have seemed too
abject for discussion. One would like to know what
Dr. Johnson would have said to any one who had
offered him a negro idol for several hundred pounds.
It would have seemed then sheer lunacy to listen to
what a negro savage had to tell us of his emotions
about the human form. And now one has to go all
the way to Chelsea in a chastened spirit and prostrate
oneself before his "stocks and stones."

We have the habit of thinking that the power to
create expressive plastic form is one of the greatest
of human achievements, and the names of great sculptors are handed down from generation to generation,
so that it seems unfair to be forced to admit that certain
nameless savages have possessed this power not only
in a higher degree than we at this moment, but than we
as a nation have ever possessed it. And yet that is
where I find myself. I have to admit that some of
these things are great sculpture—greater, I think, than
anything we produced even in the Middle Ages. Certainly they have the special qualities of sculpture in
a higher degree. They have indeed complete plastic
freedom; that is to say, these African artists really
conceive form in three dimensions. Now this is rare
in sculpture. All archaic European sculpture—Greek
and Romanesque, for instance—approaches plasticity

from the point of view of bas-relief. The statue bears traces of having been conceived as the combination of front, back, and side bas-reliefs. And this continues to make itself felt almost until the final development of the tradition. Complete plastic freedom with us seems only to come at the end of a long period, when the art has attained a high degree of representational skill and when it is generally already decadent from the point of view of imaginative significarce.

Now, the strange thing about these African sculptures is that they bear, as far as I can see, no trace of this process. Without ever attaining anything like representational accuracy they have complete freedom. The sculptors seem to have no difficulty in getting away from the two-dimensional plane. The neck and the torso are conceived as cylinders, not as masses with a square section. The head is conceived as a pear-shaped mass. It is conceived as a single whole, not arrived at by approach from the mask, as with almost all primitive European art. The mask itself is conceived as a concave plane cut out of this otherwise perfectly unified mass.

And here we come upon another curious difference between negro sculpture and our own, namely, that the emphasis is utterly different. Our emphasis has always been affected by our preferences for certain forms which appeared to us to mark the nobility of man. Thus we shrink from giving the head its full development; we like to lengthen the legs and generally to force the form into a particular type. These preferences seem to be dictated not by a plastic bias, but by our reading of the physical symbols of certain inner qualities which we admire in our kind, such, for instance, as agility, a commanding presence, or a pensive brow. The negro, it seems, either has no such preferences, or his preferences happen to coincide more nearly with what his feeling for pure plastic design would dictate. For instance, the length, thinness, and isolation of our limbs render them extremely refractory to fine plastic treatment, and the negro scores heavily by his willingness to reduce the limbs to a succession of ovoid masses sometimes scarcely longer than they are broad. Generally speaking, one may say that his plastic sense leads him to give its utmost amplitude and relief to all the protuberant parts of the body, and to get thereby an extraordinarily emphatic and impressive sequence of planes. So far from clinging to two dimensions, as we tend to do, he actually underlines, as it were, the three-dimensionalness of his forms. It is in some such way, I suspect, that he manages to give to his forms their disconcerting vitality, the suggestion that they make of being not mere echoes of actual figures, but of possessing an inner life of their own. If the negro artist wanted to make people believe in the potency of his idols he certainly set about it in the right way.

Besides the logical comprehension of plastic form which the negro shows, he has also an exquisite taste in his handling of material. No doubt in this matter his endless leisure has something to do with the marvellous finish of these works. An instance of this is seen in the treatment of the tattoo cicatrices. These are always rendered in relief, which means that the artist has cut away the whole surface around them. I fancy most sculptors would have found some less laborious method of interpreting these markings. But this patient elaboration of the surface is characteristic of most of these works. It is seen to perfection in a wooden cup covered all over with a design of faces and objects that look like clubs in very low relief. The *galbe* of this cup shows a subtlety and refinement of taste comparable to that of the finest Oriental craftsmen.

It is curious that a people who produced such great artists did not produce also a culture in our sense of the word. This shows that two factors are necessary to produce the cultures which distinguish civilised peoples. There must be, of course, the creative artist, but there must also be the power of conscious critical appreciation and comparison. If we imagined such an apparatus of critical appreciation as the Chinese have possessed from the earliest times applied to this negro art, we should have no difficulty in recognising its singular beauty. We should never have been tempted to regard it as savage or unrefined. It is for want of a conscious critical sense and the intellectual powers of comparison and classification that the negro has failed to create one of the great cultures of the world, and not from any lack of the creative æsthetic impulse, nor from lack of the most exquisite sensibility and the finest taste. No doubt, also, the lack of such a critical standard to support him leaves the artist much more at the mercy of any outside influence. It is likely enough that the negro artist, although capable of such profound imaginative understanding of form, would accept our cheapest illusionist art with humble enthusiasm.

ANCIENT AMERICAN ART[1]

NOTHING in the history of our Western civilisation is more romantic nor for us more tantalising than the story of the discovery and the wanton destruction of the ancient civilisations of America. Here were two complex civilisations which had developed in complete independence of the rest of the world; even so completely independent of each other that, for all their general racial likeness, they took on almost opposite characters. If only we could know these alternative efforts of the human animal to come to terms with nature and himself with something like the same fullness with which we know the civilisations

[1] Burlington Magazine, 1918.

of Greece and Rome, what might we not learn about
the fundamental necessities of mankind ? They would
have been for us the opposite point of our orbit; they
would have given us a parallax from which we might
have estimated the movements of that dimmest and
most distant phenomenon, the social nature of man.
And as it is, what scraps of ill-digested and ill-arranged
information and what fragments of ruined towns have
to suffice us ! Still, so fascinating is the subject that
we owe Mr. Joyce[1] a debt of gratitude for the careful
and thorough accumulation of all the material which
the archæological remains afford. These by themselves
would be only curious or beautiful as the case may
be; their full value and significance can only come out
when they are illustrated by whatever is known of
their place in the historical sequence of the civilisations.
Mr. Joyce gives us what is known of the outlines of
Mexican and Peruvian history as far as it can be de-
ciphered from the early accounts of Spanish invaders
and from the original documents, and he brings the
facts thus established to bear on the antiquities. Unfortunately for the reader of these books, the story
is terribly involved and complicated even when it is
not dubious. Thus in Mexico we have to deal with
an almost inextricable confusion of tribes and languages
having much in common, but each interpreting their
common mythology and religion in a special manner.
Even Greek mythology, which we once seemed to
know fairly well, takes on under the pressure of modern
research an unfamiliar formlessness—becomes indistinct
and shifting in its outlines; and the various civilisations
of Mexico each with its innumerable gods and goddesses
with varying names and varying attributes, produce on
the mind a sense of bewildering and helpless wonder,

[1] Thomas A. Joyce, (1) "South American Archæology,"
London (Macmillan), 1912; (2) "Mexican Archæology," London
(Lee Warner), 1914; (3) "Central American Archæology,"
London and New York (Putnam), 1916.

and still more a sense of pervading horror at the underlying nature of the human imagination. For one
quality emerges in all the different aspects of their
religions, its hideous inhumanity and cruelty, its direct
inspiration of all the most ingenious tortures both
in peace and war—above all, the close alliance between
religion and war and going with both of these the worship of suffering as an end in itself. Only at one point
in this nightmare of inhumanity do we get a momentary
sense of pleasure—itself a savage one—that is in the
knowledge that at certain sacred periods the priests,
whose main business was the torturing of others, were
themselves subjected to the purificatory treatment.
A bas-relief in the British Museum shows with grim
realism the figure of a kneeling priest with pierced
tongue, pulling a rope through the hole. Under such
circumstances one would at least hesitate to accuse
the priesthood of hypocrisy.

When we turn to Peru the picture is less grim. The
Incas do not seem to have been so abjectly religious as the
Aztecs; they had at least abolished human sacrifice, which
the Aztecs practised on a colossal scale, and though the
tyranny of the governing classes was more highly organised, it was inspired by a fairly humane conception.

But we must leave the speculations on such general
questions, which are as regards these books incidental
to the main object, and turn to the consideration of
the archæological remains and the investigation of
their probable sequence and dating.

Our attitude to the artistic remains of these civilisations has a curious history. The wonder of the Spanish
invaders at the sight of vast and highly organised
civilisations where only savagery was expected has never
indeed ceased, but the interest in their remains has
changed from time to time. The first emotion they
excited besides wonder was the greed of the conquerors
for the accumulated treasure. Then among the more

cultivated Spaniards supervened a purely scientific
curiosity to which we owe most of our knowledge of
the indigenous legend and history. Then came the
question of origins, which is still as fascinating and
unsettled as ever, and to the belief that the Mexicans
were the lost ten tribes of Israel we owe Lord Kings-
borough's monumental work in nine volumes on
Mexican antiquities. To such odd impulses perhaps,
rather than to any serious appreciation of their artistic
merits, we owe the magnificent collection of Mexican
antiquities in the British Museum. Indeed, it is only
in this country that, after contemplating them from
every other point of view, we have begun to look at
them seriously as works of art. Probably the first works
to be admitted to this kind of consideration were the
Peruvian pots in the form of highly realistic human
heads and figures.[1]

Still more recently we have come to recognise the
beauty of Aztec and Maya sculpture, and some of our
modern artists have even gone to them for inspiration.
This is, of course, one result of the general æsthetic
awakening which has followed on the revolt against
the tyranny of the Græco-Roman tradition.

Both in Mexico and Peru we have to deal with
at least two, possibly four, great cultures, each over-
thrown in turn by the invasion of less civilised, more
warlike tribes, who gradually adopt the general scheme
of the older civilisation. In Mexico there is no doubt
about the superiority, from an artistic point of view, of the
earlier culture—the Aztecs had everything to learn from
the Maya, and they never rose to the level of their predecessors. The relation is, in fact, curiously like that of
Rome to Greece. Unfortunately we have to learn almost
all we know of Maya culture through their Aztec conquerors, but the ruins of Yucatan and Guatemala are
by far the finest and most complete vestiges left to us.

[1] The Burlington Magazine, vol. xvii., p. 22 (April, 1910).

In Peru also we find in the Tihuanaco gateway a monument of some pre-Inca civilisation, and one that in regard to the art of sculpture far surpasses anything that the later culture reveals. It is of special interest, moreover, for its strong stylistic likeness to the Maya sculpture of Yucatan. This similarity prompts the interesting speculation whether the earlier civilisations of the two continents had either a common origin or points of contact, whereas the Inca and Aztec cultures seem to drift entirely apart. The Aztecs carry on at a lower level the Maya art of sculpture, whereas the Incas seem to drop sculpture almost entirely, a curious fact in view of the ambitious nature of their architectural and engineering works. One seems to guess that the comparatively humane socialistic tyranny of the Incas developed more and more along purely practical lines, whilst the hideous religiosity of the Aztecs left a certain freedom to the imaginative artist.

In looking at the artistic remains of so remote and strange a civilisation one sometimes wonders how far one can trust one's æsthetic appreciation to interpret truly the feelings which inspired it. In certain works one cannot doubt that the artist felt just as we feel in appreciating his work. This must, I think, hold on the one hand of the rich ornamental arabesques of Maya buildings or the marvellous inlaid feather and jewel work of either culture; and on the other hand, when we look at the caricatural realistic figures of Truxillo pottery we need scarcely doubt that the artist's intention agrees with our appreciation, for such a use of the figure is more or less common to all civilisations. But when we look at the stylistic sculpture of Maya and Aztec art, are we, one wonders, reading in an intention which was not really present? One wonders, for instance, how far external and accidental factors may not have entered in to help produce what seems to us the perfect and delicate balance between representational

and purely formal consideration. Whether the artist
was not held back both by ritualistic tradition and
the difficulty of his medium from pushing further the
actuality of his presentation—whether, in fact, the
artist deplored or himself approved just that reticence
which causes our admiration. At times Maya sculpture has a certain similarity to Indian religious sculptural
reliefs, particularly in the use of flat surfaces entirely
incrusted with ornaments in low relief; but on the whole
the comparison is all in favour of the higher æsthetic
sensibility of the Maya artists, whose co-ordination of
even the most complicated forms compares favourably
with the incoherent luxuriance of most Indian work.

In this, as in so many of its characteristics, Maya
art comes much nearer to early Chinese sculpture;
and again one wonders that such a civilisation should
have produced such sensitive and reasoned designs—
designs which seem to imply a highly developed self-
conscious æsthetic sensibility. Nor do the Maya, for
all their hieratic ritualism, seem to fall into the dead,
mechanical repetition which the endless multiplication
of religious symbols usually entails, as, for instance,
most markedly in Egyptian art. But this strange difference between what we know of Mexican civilisation and
what we might have interpreted from the art alone
is only one more instance of the isolation of the æsthetic
from all other human activities.

The sculptures of Pedras Negras, of which casts
may be seen in the British Museum, are among the
finest remains of Maya sculpture. They show at once
the extreme richness of the decorative effect and the
admirable taste with which this is co-ordinated in a plastic
whole in which the figure has its due predominance.
Though the relief of the ornamental part is kept flat and
generally square in section, it has nothing of the dryness
and tightness that such a treatment often implies.

Mr. Joyce's books are compiled with amazing in-

dustry, and contain a vast accumulation of information.
If we have a complaint, it is that for those who are
not specialists, this information is poured out in almost
too uniform a flood, with too little by way of general
ideas to enable the mind to grasp or relate them properly.
If some of the minor details of obscure proper names
had been relegated to the notes, it would have been
possible to seize the general outlines more readily.
The books are rather for reference than adapted to
consecutive reading. In his judgments on the various
speculations to which these civilisations have given
rise Mr. Joyce is, as one would expect from so careful
a scholar, cautious and negative. He does not, as far
as I remember, even allude to the theory of the Lost
Ten Tribes, but he does condescend to discuss the
theory of cultural influence from Eastern Asia which
has more than once been put forward by respectable
ethnologists. He decides against this fascinating hypothesis more definitely than one would expect—more
definitely, I should say, than the facts before us allow.
He declares, for instance, that the calendrical system
of Mexico shows no similarity with those of Eastern
Asia, whereas Dr. Lehmann gives a circumstantial
account of a very curious likeness, the almost exact
correspondence of two quite peculiar systems of reckon-
ing. My own bias in favour of the theory of Eastern
Asiatic influence is, I confess, based on what may
seem very insufficient grounds, namely, the curious
likeness of the general treatment of naturalistic forms
and the peculiar character of the stylisation of natural
forms in early Chinese and American art. It is of course
impossible to define a likeness of general character
which depends so largely on feeling, but it consists
to some extent in the predilection for straight lines and
rectangles—a spiral in nature becoming in both early
Chinese and American art a sequence of rectangular
forms with rounded corners. What is more remarkable

D

is that the further back we go in Chinese art the greater the resemblance becomes, so that a Chou bronze, or still more the carved horns which have survived from the Shang dynasty, are extraordinarily like Maya or Tihuanaco sculpture. Again, it is curious to note how near to early Chinese bronzes are the tripod vases of the Guetar Indians. All these may of course be of quite independent origin, but their similarity cannot be dismissed lightly in view of the long persistence in any civilisation of such general habits of design. Thus the general habits of design of the Cretan civilisation

persisted into Greek and even Roman and Christian art; the habits of design of Chinese artists have persisted, though through great modifications, for more than three thousand years. One other fact which may seem almost too isolated and insignificant may perhaps be put forward here. In a history of the Mormons, published in 1851, there is given a figure of an inscribed bronze (see Figure) which was dug up by the Mormons in Utah in 1843. Since Brigham Young pretended to have dug up the original book of Mormon his followers had a superstitious reverence for all such treasure trove, and probably the bronze still exists and might be worth investigation. Now this drawing, here reproduced, looks to me like an extremely bad and unintelligent reproduction of an early Chinese object, in general appearance not unlike certain early pieces of jade. It is fairly certain that at the time the Mormons discovered this, no such objects had found their way out of China, since the interest in and knowledge of this period of Chinese art is of much later growth. So it appears conceivable that the object, whatever its nature, is a relic of some early cultural invasion from Eastern Asia. The physical possibilities of such invasions from the Far East certainly seem to be under-estimated by Mr. Joyce.

THE MUNICH EXHIBITION OF MOHAMMEDAN ART [1]

IT would be hard to exaggerate the importance of this exhibition for those who are interested in the history not alone of Oriental but of European art. One of the most fascinating of the problems that present themselves to the art historian is that of the origins of mediæval art. Until we understand more or less completely how in the dim centuries of the later Empire and early middle age the great transformation of Græco-Roman into mediæval art was accomplished, we cannot quite understand the Renaissance itself, nor even the form which the whole modern art of Europe has come in the course of centuries to assume. And on this problem the Munich exhibition throws many illuminating side-lights. Early Mohammedan art is seen here to be a meeting-point of many influences. There are still traces of the once widespread Hellenistic tradition, though this is seen to be retreating before the refluent wave of aboriginal ideas. Sassanid art had already been the outcome of these contending forces, and the pre-eminence of Sassanid art in forming early Mohammedan styles is clearly brought out in this exhibition. Then there is a constant exchange with Byzantium, and finally continual waves of influence, sometimes fer-

tilising, sometimes destructive, from that great reservoir
of Central Asian civilisation, the importance of which
is now at last being gradually revealed to us by the
discoveries of Dr. Stein, Drs. Lecoq and Grunwedel,
and M. Pelliot.

And through this great clearing-house of early Mohammedan art there are signs of influences passing
from West to East. The most striking example is that
of the plate in cloisonnée enamel from the Landes
Museum at Innsbruck. Here we have the one certain
example of Mohammedan cloisonnée enamel established
by its dedication to a prince of the Orthokid dynasty
of the twelfth century. It is extraordinary that this
solitary example should alone have survived from what
must, judging from the technical excellence of this
specimen, have once been a flourishing craft. The general
effect of the intricate pattern of animal forms upon a
whitish ground suggests, on the one hand, the earliest
examples of Limoges enamels, and on the other the early
Chinese, and there can be little doubt that the Chinese
did in fact derive their knowledge of cloisonnée, which
they themselves called "Western ware," from these
early Mohammedan craftsmen, who had themselves
learned the technique from Byzantium.

But on the whole the stream of influence is in the
opposite direction, from East to West, and one realises
at Munich that in the great period of artistic discovery
and formation of styles the near East and the West
were developing in closest contact and harmony.
Indeed the most fertile, if not actually the most resplend-
dent, period of both arts was attained whilst they were
still almost indistinguishable. If it were not for the
habit of these early Mohammedan craftsmen of interweaving inscriptions into their designs, a habit which
endears them quite especially to art-historians, how
many works of Oriental manufacture would have been
ascribed to Europe ? In spite of these inscriptions,

indeed, such an authority as M. Babelon has sought to place to the account of Western artists the superb cut crystal vessels, of which the noblest example is the inscribed ewer of the tenth century in the treasury of S. Mark's. Or take again the textiles. In the exhibition there are a number of fragments of textiles of the tenth to the twelfth centuries, in which the general principle of design is the same; for the most part the surface is covered by circular reserves in which severely conventionalised figures of hunters, lions, or monsters are placed in pairs symmetrically confronted. Only minute study has enabled specialists to say that some were made in Sassanid Persia, some in Byzantium, some in Sicily, and some in Western Europe. The dominant style in all these is again derived from Sassanid art. And here once more one must note the strange recrudescence after so long of Assyrian types and motives, and its invasion of Western Europe, through Byzantium, Sicily, and Spain.

What strikes us most in comparing Græco-Roman art with the new art which gradually emerges in the middle ages is that, on the one hand, we have a series of decorative designs never so remarkable for vitality as for their elegance, and become by the time of the Roman Empire only a little less perfunctory and mechanical than the patterns of modern times; and on the other hand an art in which the smallest piece of pattern-making shows a tense vitality even in its most purely geometrical manifestations, and the figure is used with a new dramatic expressiveness unhindered by the artist's ignorance of actual form. Now in the splendid photographs of the Sassanid rock carvings which Dr. Sarre has taken and which are exposed at Munich, we can see something of this process of the creation of the new vital system of design. In the earlier reliefs, those of the time of Sapor, we have, it is true, a certain theatrical splendour of pose and setting, but in the actual forms some flaccidity and inflation. The artists who wrought them show still the predominance of the worn-out Hellenistic tradition which spread in Alexander's wake over Asia. In the stupendous relief of Chosroes at Tak-i-Bostan, on the other hand, we have all the dramatic energy, the heraldic splendour of the finest mediæval art, and the source of this new inspiration is seen to be the welling up once more of the old indigenous Mesopotamian art. We have once more that singular feeling for stress, for muscular tension, and for dramatic oppositions which distinguish the bas-reliefs of Babylon and Nineveh from all other artistic expressions of the antique world. It would be possible by the help of exhibits at Munich to trace certain Assyrian forms right through to Mediæval European art. Take, for instance, the lion heads on the pre-Babylonian mace from Goudea in the Louvre; one finds a precisely similar convention for the lion head on the Sassanid repoussé metalwork found in Russia. Once again it occurs in the superb carved rock crystal waterspout lent by the Karlsruhe Museum (Room 54), and one finds it again on the font of Lincoln Cathedral and in the lions that support the doorway columns of Italian cathedrals. In all these there is a certain community of style, a certain way of symbolising the leonine nature which one may look for in vain in Greek and Græco-Roman art.

Even if this seem too forced an interpretation of facts, it is none the less clear that everywhere in early Mohammedan art this recrudescence of Assyrian forms may be traced, and that their influence was scarcely less upon Europe than upon the near East. Dr. Sarre has taken a tracing of the pattern which is represented in low relief upon the robes of Chosroes in the Tak-i-Bostan relief. In South Kensington Museum there is an almost identical piece of silk brocade which actually comes from the ruins of Khorsabad, and in the same museum one may find more than one Byzantine imitation of this design and closely similar ones made in Sicily; and the conventional winged monster which forms the basis of these designs has a purely Assyrian air.

In Egypt, too, it would seem that there was before the Arab invasion a marked recrudescence of indigenous native design which enabled the Coptic craftsmen gradually to transform the motives given to them by Roman conquerors into something entirely non-Hellenistic. And the incredible beauty of the Fatimite textiles of the tenth, eleventh, and twelfth centuries, of which a few precious relics are shown in Room 17, preserve something, especially in the bird forms, of this antique derivation.

But to return once more to Sassanid art. The specimens from the Hermitage and Prince Bobrinsky's collections form an object lesson of extraordinary interest in the development of early Mohammedan art. They have inherited and still retain that extreme realisation of massive splendour, that fierce assertion of form and positive statement of relief which belongs to the art of the great primitive Empires, and most of all to the art of Mesopotamia, and yet they already adumbrate the forms of Mohammedan art into which they pass by insensible degrees. Here, too, we find vestiges of the dying Hellenistic tradition. One of Prince Bobrinsky's bronzes, a great plate, has, for instance, a design composed of classic vases, from which spring stems which bend round into a series of circles, a design which might almost be matched as regards form, though not as regards spirit, in the wall decorations of Pompeii. Or take again the superb repoussé silver plate representing a Sassanid king spearing a lion. Here the floating drapery of the king and the edge of his tunic show a deliberately schematised rendering of the traditional folds of the Greek peplos. But how

much more Assyrian than Greek is the whole effect
—the dramatic tension of the figures expressed by
an emphasis on all the lines of muscular effort, as in
the legs of the horse and the lions! How Assyrian,
too, is the feeling for relief, and the predilection for
imbricated or closely set parallel lines as in the lions'
manes! In the conventional rock under one of the
lions one seems to see also a hint of Chinese forms.

Still more Assyrian is another plate. the arrangement of which recalls the reliefs of Assurbanipal or
Sennacherib, and yet already there are forms which
anticipate Mohammedan art; the gate of the city,
its crenelations, and the forms of the helmets of the
soldiers, all have an air of similarity with far later
Mohammedan types. Another plate shows a Sassanid
king regaling himself with wine and music, and gives
already more than a hint of the favourite designs of
the Rhages potters or the bronze workers of Mossoul.

Among Prince Bobrinsky's bronzes which were
found in the Caucasus is a late Sassanid aquamanile
in the form of a bird. It is already almost Mohammedan, though retaining something of the extreme
solidity and weight of earlier art. Once more, in the
aggressive schematisation of the form of the tail and
the suggestion of feathers by a series of deeply marked
parallel lines, we get a reminiscence of Assyrian art,
while in the treatment of the crest there is the more
florid interweaving of curves which adumbrate not only
Mohammedan but Indian forms.

In the aquamanile in the form of a horse, the Sassanid
influence is still predominant, but there can be no
doubt that this is already Mohammedan, probably of
the eighth or ninth century. We have already here the
characteristics of Fatimite bronzes, of which a few
specimens are shown at Munich. The great griffin
of Pisa could not, of course, be moved from the Campo
Santo, nor are the two specimens in the Louvre shown,

but the stag from the Bavarian National Museum is there and affords a most interesting comparison with Prince Bobrinsky's horse. Both have the same large generalisation of form, and in both we have the curious effect of solidity and mass produced by the shortened hind legs, with the half-squatting movement to which that gives rise.

The Bobrinsky horse is obviously more primitive, and probably indicates the beginnings of a school of bronze plastic in Mesopotamia nearly parallel to that of Egypt. This school, however, never developed as fully along sculptural lines, and at a comparatively early date abandoned sculpture for the art of bronze inlay, of which Mossoul was the great centre in the twelfth and thirteenth centuries. In the incised designs on the horse we have an example of the early forms of the palmette ornament and of the interlacing curves which form the basis of most subsequent Mohammedan patterns. Within the reserves formed by the *intreccie* are small figures, of which one—that of a man seated and playing the lute—can just be made out in the reproduction. It is already typical of the figure design which the Mohammedan artists developed in the twelfth and thirteenth centuries.

It shows the peculiar characteristics of all the art produced for the Fatimite court, its exquisite perfection and refinement of taste, its minuteness of detail and finish together with a large co-ordination of parts, a rhythmic feeling for contour and the sequence of planes, which have scarcely ever been equalled. And all these qualities of refinement, almost of sophistication, which Fatimite art possesses do not, as we see here, destroy the elementary imaginative feeling for the vitality of animal forms. With this Mesopotamian example we may compare the lion from the Kassel Museum. This is a splendid example of Fatimite sculpture. It causes one to regret that Mohammedan artists

so soon abandoned an art for which they show such
extraordinary aptitude. The lion which comes from
the Kassel Museum has already been published by
M. Migeon,[1] but is of such rare beauty and interest in
relation to the Sassanid works here described that it
seemed desirable to reproduce it again. In the case
in which this masterpiece of Mohammedan sculpture
is shown there is also seen the celebrated lion which
once belonged to the painter Fortuny. Noble though
this is in general conception, the coarseness of its
workmanship and the want of subtlety in its proportions, in comparison with the Kassel lion, makes
it evident that it is not from the same school of Egyptian
craftsmen, but probably of Spanish origin.

Yet another of the Bobrinsky bronzes of about the
same date as the horse is already typically Mohammedan as may be seen by the leaf forms and the *intreccie*
of the crest, but how much of the antique Sassanid
proportions and sense of relief is still retained ! It is
believed to be from Western Turkestan and of the
eighth or ninth century. One must suppose that Sassanid
forms travelled North and East as well as South and
West, and helped in the formation of that Central
Asian art which becomes the dominant factor in the
later centuries of Mohammedan, more especially of
Persian, art.

Before leaving the question of Sassanid influences
I must mention the series of bronze jugs in the Bobrinsky
and Sarre collections. The general form is obviously
derived from classic originals, but they have a peculiar
spout of a rectangular shape placed at right angles on
the top of the main opening. The effect of this is to give
two openings, one for pouring the water in, the other
for pouring it out at right angles. Now in the early
Mossoul water-jugs we see numerous examples of

[1] G. Migeon, *Gazette des Beaux Arts*, June, 1905, and
"Manuel d'Art Musulman," p. 226.

what are clearly derivations of this form passing by gradual degrees into the familiar neck with spout attached but not separated, which is typical of later Mohammedan water-jugs. This evolution can be traced step by step in the Munich Exhibition, and leaves no doubt of the perfect continuity of Sassanid and Mohammedan forms.[1]

One of the features of early Mohammedan art is the vitality of its floral and geometrical ornament, the system of which is uniformly spread throughout the Mohammedan world. The question of where and how this system of ornament arose is not easily solved, but there are indications that Egypt was the place of its earliest development. Its characteristic forms seem certainly derived from the universal palmette of Græco-Roman decoration. The palmette, so rigid, unvarying and frequently so lifeless in the hands of Græco-Roman artists, became the source of the flexible and infinitely varied systems of Mohammedan design, so skilfully interwoven, so subtly adapted to their purpose, that the supremacy of Mohammedan art in this particular has been recognised and perpetuated in the word Arabesque. It is curious to note that the history of this development is almost a repetition of what occurred many centuries before in the formation of the system of Celtic ornament. There, too, the Greek palmette was the point of departure. The Celtic bronze-workers adopted a cursive abbreviation of it which allowed of an almost too unrestrained flexibility in their patterns, but one peculiarly adapted to their bronze technique. In the case of Mohammedan art it would seem that the change from the palmette was

[1] I cannot help calling attention, though without any attempt at explaining it, to the striking similarity to these Sassanid and early Mohammedan water-jugs shown by an example of Sung pottery lent by Mr. Eumorfopoulos to the recent exhibition at the Burlington Fine Arts Club, Case A, No. 43. Here a very similar form of spout is modelled into a phœnix's head.

effected by Coptic wood-carvers and by the artists who
decorated in plaster the earliest Egyptian mosques.
Indeed, one may suspect that the transformation of
Græco-Roman ornament had already been initiated
by Coptic workers in pre-Mohammedan times. One
or two exhibits of Coptic reliefs in woodwork in
Room 48 show how far this process had already gone.
The Coptic wood-carvers arrived at an extremely
simple and economical method of decoration by in-
cisions with a gouge, each ending in a spiral curve,
and so set as to leave in relief a sequence of forms
resembling a half-palmette, and at times approaching
very closely to the characteristic interlacing "trumpet"
forms of Celtic ornament. A similar method was
employed with even greater freedom and with a surprising richness and variety of effect in the plaster
decorations of the earliest mosques, such as that of
Ibn Tulun. In this way there was developed a singularly easy and rhythmic manner of filling any given
space with interlaced and confluent forms suited to
the caligraphic character of Mohammedan design.
It cannot be denied that in course of time it pandered
to the besetting sin of the oriental craftsman, his in-
tolerable patience and thoughtless industry, and became
in consequence as dead in its mere intricacy and complexity as the Græco-Roman original in its frigid
correctness. The periods of creation in ornamental
design seem indeed to be even rarer than those of
creation in the figurative arts, and if the greater part
of Mohammedan art shows, along with increasing
technical facility, a constant degradation in ornamental
design it is no exception to a universal rule. At any
rate, up to the end of the thirteenth century its vitality
was as strong and its adaptability even greater than
the ornamental design of Christian Europe.

The design based on the half-palmette adapted
itself easily to other materials than wood and plaster.

In an even more cursive form it was used alike by miniaturists and the closely allied painters on pottery. Of the former a good instance is that of a manuscript of Dioscorides, written and painted by Abdullah ben el-Fadhl in the year 1223 A.D. It is of Mesopotamian origin and shows in the decorative treatment of the figures a close affinity with the painting on contemporary pottery from Rakka. It is surprising how much character and even humour the artist gives to figures which are conceived in a purely calligraphic and abstract manner, and what richness and nobility of style there is in the singularly economical and rapid indications of brocaded patterns in the robes. Here we see how, in the hands of the miniaturists, the half-palmette ornament becomes even more cursive and flexible, more readily adapted to any required space than in the hands of the wood-carver and plasterer.

The whole of the figure-design of this period, as seen in the pottery of Rakka, Rhages, and Sultana-bad, shows the same characteristics. It is all calligraphic rather than naturalistic, but it is notable how much expression is attained within the flexible formula which these Mohammedan artists had evolved. The requirements of the potter's craft stimulated the best elements of such a school of draughtsmanship, and for their power of creating an illusion of real existence by the sheer swiftness and assurance of their rhthym, few draughtsmen had surpassed the unknown masters who threw their indications of scenes from contemporary life upon the fragile bowls and lustred cups of early Syrian and Persian pottery.

It is generally believed now that not only in ceramics and metal-work, but even in glass, Fatimite culture was pre-eminent. Probably no such collection of enamelled oriental glass has ever been brought together as that at Munich.

An example of glass of Egyptian origin bearing the

date A.D. 737, belonging to Dr. Fouquet, shows how
early the manufacture of glass was already established
in Egypt. To Egypt, too, must be ascribed the splendid
crystals and carved glass-work in which the Munich
Exhibition is particularly rich. One of these is the so-
called Hedwig glass from the Rijksmuseum at Amster-
dam. It has two finely conventionalised lions and
eagles which resemble the types of Fatimite sculpture.
It is described by Migeon ("Manuel," p. 378) as being
of moulded glass, but the design is probably cut on the
wheel in the manner employed for rock-crystal. Among
the examples of carved crystal one of the finest is the
less well-known example of a water-spout in the shape
of a lion's head, lent by the Karlsruhe Museum. In
all these figures the distinctive quality of Fatimite art,
its combination of massive grandeur of design with
extreme refinement, are apparent.

None the less, the evidence in favour of Syrian and
Mesopotamian centres of glass-industry is very strong,
and if many of the pieces, especially the earliest ones,
are still relegated to Egypt, some of the finest are still
ascribed, though on no very conclusive grounds, to
the Syrian workshops. The finest of these belong to
the late twelfth and early thirteenth centuries, and,
generally speaking, the work of the fourteenth century
shows a decline. Perhaps the most splendid specimen
known is the large bottle from the treasury of
S. Stephen's, Vienna. The glass in this and the kindred
piece from the same place shows a peculiar brownish-
yellow tone almost of the colour of honey, which gives
the most perfect background to the enamelled figure-
decoration. In the choice of subjects with a predominance of scenes from the chase there is undoubtedly
a considerable resemblance to the scenes on the en-
crusted bronze work of Mossoul, and this, so far as it
goes, makes in favour of a Syrian origin. But whatever
their origin, the finest of these pieces show a decorative

splendour and a perfection of taste which have assured their appreciation from the days of the Crusaders. Already in the inventory of Charles V. of France such pieces, frequently mounted on silver stands, figure among the King's choicest treasures. Nor was the appreciation of this beautiful craft confined to Europe. One of the many proofs of a continual interchange between the Mohammedan and Chinese civilisations is seen in the number of examples of this glass which have come from China. In Munich there is a magnificent bowl lent by Dr. Sarre which is of Chinese provenance, and numerous other pieces have been recorded.

The collection of incrusted bronzes at Munich is extremely rich, ranging from the twelfth-century work, in which plastic relief is still used, accompanied by sparse incrustations of red copper upon the almost strawy yellow bronze, to the fourteenth and fifteenth-century work, in which plastic relief has altogether disappeared, and elaborate incrustations of silver and even gold give to the surface an extreme profusion of delicate interwoven traceries. Here, too, the earliest work shows the finest sense of design. The specimen from the Piet Latauderie collection still retains in its relief of stylistic animals a feeling for mass and grandeur inherited from Sassanid metal-workers, and the incrustations, though exquisitely wrought, are kept in due subordination to the general design. Some of the thirteenth-century pieces, though already tending to too great intricacy, still attain to a finely co-ordinated effect by the use of reserves filled with boldly designed figures. Some of the best of these contain scenes borrowed from Christian mythology, among which I may mention, as a superb example, the great bowl belonging to the Duc d'Arenberg.

I have alluded at various points to the influence of Chinese art upon Mohammedan. Among the most decisive and curious instances of this is a bronze mirror with the signs of the Zodiac in relief. Round the edge is an inscription of dedication to one of the Orthokid princes. It is of Mesopotamian workmanship. Here the derivation from Chinese mirrors, which date back to Han times, is unmistakable, and is seen in every detail, even to the griffin head in the centre, pierced to allow of the string by which it was carried.

GIOTTO[1]
THE CHURCH OF S. FRANCESCO AT ASSISI

WE find abundant evidences in studying early Christian art that Christianity at its origin exercised no new stimulating influence upon its development, but if it were claimed for the Franciscan movement that it brought about the great outburst of Italian art the position would be harder to refute: and indeed what S. Francis accomplished, the literal acceptance by official Christendom of Christ's teaching, was tantamount to the foundation of a new religion, and the heresy of some of his followers, who regarded his as a final dispensation superseding that of the New Testament, can scarcely have seemed unreasonable to those who witnessed the change in the temper of society which his example brought about. S. Francis was the great orthodox heretic. What he effected

[1] The following, from the Monthly Review, 1901, is, perhaps more than any other article here reprinted, at variance with the more recent expressions of my æsthetic ideas. It will be seen that great emphasis is laid on Giotto's expression of the dramatic idea in his pictures. I still think this is perfectly true so far as it goes, nor do I doubt that an artist like Giotto did envisage such an expression. I should be inclined to disagree wherever in this article there appears the assumption not only that the dramatic idea may have inspired the artist to the creation of his form, but that the value of the form for us is bound up with recognition of the dramatic idea. It now seems to me possible by a more searching analysis of our experience in front of a work of art to disentangle our reaction to pure form from our reaction to its implied associated ideas.

within the bounds of the Church, for a time at all events, was only accomplished for later times by a rupture with the Papal power. He established the idea of the equality of all men before God and the immediate relationship of the individual soul to the Deity. He enabled every man to be his own priest. To the fervour, with which these ideas were grasped by his countrymen we may ascribe to some extent the extreme individualism of the Italian Renaissance, the absence of the barriers of social caste to the aspirations of the individual and the passionate assertion on his part of the right to the free use of all his activities. No doubt the individualism of, say, a Sigismondo Malatesta in the fifteenth century was very different from anything which S. Francis would have approved; none the less such a view of life was rendered possible by the solvent action of his teaching on the fixed forms of society.

But of more immediate importance to our purpose is the æsthetic element in S. Francis' teaching. To say that in his actions S. Francis aimed at artistic effect would perhaps give a wrong impression of his character, but it is true that his conception of holiness was almost as much an æsthetic as a moral one. To those who know S. Bonaventura's life a number of stories will suggest themselves, which indicate a perfectly harmonious attitude to life rather than a purely moral one: stories such as that of the sheep which was given to him, and which he received joyfully because of its simplicity and innocence, "and holding it in his hands he admonished it to be intent to praise God and to keep itself from offending the brethren; and the sheep observed fully the commandment of the Blessed Francis, and when it heard the brethren singing in the choir ran thither quickly, and without any teaching bent before the altar of the Blessed Virgin and bleated, as though it had human reason."

S. Francis, the "Jongleur de Dieu," was actually

a poet before his conversion, and his whole life had the pervading unity and rhythm of a perfect work of art. Not that he was a conscious artist. The whole keynote of the Franciscan teaching was its spontaneity, but his feelings for moral and æsthetic beauty were intimately united. Indeed, his life, like the Italian art which in a sense arose from it, like the Gothic French art which was a simultaneous expression of the same spirit, implies an attitude, as rare in life as in art, in which spiritual and sensuous beauty are so inextricably interwoven that instead of conflicting they mutually intensify their effects.

Not only was the legend of S. Francis' life full of suggestions of poetical and artistic material, but his followers rewrote the New Testament from the Franciscan point of view, emphasising the poetical and dramatic elements of the story. In particular they shifted the focus of interest by making the relationship of the Virgin to her son the central motive of the whole. It will be seen that Italian artists down to Raphael turned rather to the Franciscan than the Vulgate version.[1] In fact, S. Bonaventura and the great poet of the movement, the cultivated and ecstatic Jacopone di Todi, did for the Christian legend very much what Pindar did for classical mythology; without altering the doctrine they brought into full relief its human and poetical significance.

It is not surprising, then, to find that the great church at Assisi, built with all the magnificence that the whole of Italy could contribute to honouring the spouse of Divine Poetry, should be the cradle of the new art of Italy—the neo-Christian of Franciscan art, as we might almost call it.

The lower church of S. Francesco was probably decorated almost immediately after the building was finished, between 1240 and 1250, but these early works

[1] *Cf.* H. Thode: "Franz von Assisi."

are almost obliterated by a second decoration undertaken after 1300. We must therefore turn to the upper church, the paintings of which were probably completed before 1300, as the chief source of our knowledge of the emergence of the new Italian style. It was there that the Italian genius first attained to self-expression in the language of monumental painting—a language which no other nation of modern Europe has ever been able to command except in rare and isolated instances.

And here we plunge at once into a very difficult, perhaps an insoluble problem: who were the painters who carried out this immense scheme of decoration? The archives of the church have been searched in vain, and we are left with a sentence of Ghiberti's commentary, and Vasari, who here proves an uncertain guide, so that we are thrown chiefly on the resources of internal evidence.

The paintings of the upper church may be briefly enumerated thus: In the choir are faint remains of frescoes of the life of the Virgin: in the right transept a Crucifixion and other subjects almost obliterated; in the left transept another Crucifixion, better preserved, and archangels in the triforium. The nave is divided into an upper and lower series; the upper series contains scenes of the Old and New Testaments, the lower is devoted to the legend of S. Francis, and in alternate vaults of the roof are paintings of single figures.

It would be out of place to discuss all these frescoes in detail, but it may be worth while to select certain typical ones, around which the rest may be grouped, and see how far they bear out what little documentary and traditional authority we have.

We will begin with the Crucifixion of the left transept, which is clearly by an artist of decided and marked personality. It is certainly less pleasing and less accomplished than the works of the later Byzantine school, and in spite of certain motives, such as the floating drapery of the Christ, which show Byzantine reminiscences, it is derived in the main from the native Italian tradition. This is shown in the stumpy proportions of the figures and the crude, not to say hideous, realism of the faces of the crowd. The classical origin of the tradition is still traceable in the sandalled feet and the reminiscence of the toga in some of the draperies. But the chief interest lies in the serious attempt made by the artist to give dramatic reality to the scene in a way never attempted by the less human Byzantines. The action of the Magdalen throwing up both arms in despair is really impressive, and this is a more vivacious rendering of a gesture traditional in Western early Christian art; an instance occurs in the fifth-century MS. of Genesis at Vienna. But the artist shows his originality more in the expressive and sometimes beautiful poses of the weeping angels and the natural movements of the Virgin and S. John.

Very nearly allied to this are the archangels of the triforium, and some of the frescoes of the upper scenes in the nave, such as the Nativity and the Betrayal. These belong to the same group, though they are not necessarily by the master of the Crucifixion himself.

As we proceed along the nave, still keeping to the upper series, we come upon another distinct personality, whose work is typified in the Deception of Isaac. In certain qualities this master is not altogether unlike the master of the Crucifixion. Like him, he replaces the purely schematic linear rendering of drapery by long streaks of light and dark paint, so arranged as to give the idea of actual modelling in relief. But he does this not only with greater naturalism, but with a greatly increased sense of pure beauty. The painting is not hieratic and formal as the Byzantine would have made it, nor has it that overstrained attempt at dramatic vehemence which we saw in the Crucifixion. The faces have remarkable beauty, and throughout there is a

sense of placid and dignified repose which is rare in
mediæval work. It is, in fact, decidedly classical, and
classical, too, in a sense different from the vague reminiscences of classic origin which permeate early Christian
art, and were faintly echoed in the Crucifixion. Rachel
especially, with her full, well-rounded eyes, wide apart
and set deep in their sockets, her straight nose and
small mouth, might almost have come straight from a
Pompeian picture.

The hair, too, instead of being in tangled masses,
as in the Crucifixion, or rendered by parallel lines, as in
the Sacrifice of Isaac, is drawn into elegantly disposed
curls, which yet have something of the quality of hair,
and which remind us of the treatment in classic bronzes.

The last vault of the nave, with the Doctors of the
Church, is by an artist who is extremely similar to
the last, and clearly belongs to the same group. The
level brows nearly meeting over the bridge of the nose,
the straight profile and the curled hair show the similarity, as does also the drapery. The classic tendencies
of this artist may be seen in the amorini caryatides in
the extreme corners of the spandrill, while the decoration
of one of the arches of the church by the same hand
has, arising from an urn of pure classic design, a foliated
scroll-work, in which centaurs disport themselves.

In the lower series representing the Life of S. Francis
we are at once struck by the resemblances to the last
two paintings. The Pope, who is approving the rule
of S. Francis, is almost a repetition of one of the Doctors
of the Church. We have the same peculiar drapery
with shiny, slippery, high lights, broadly washed on
in well-disposed folds. The faces too, though they
are more individual and far more expressive, are,
nevertheless, built on the same lines. They have similar
straight profiles, the same deeply cut level brows,
which tend to meet in a line across the nose. The
general impression it makes is that it is by a younger

artist than the master of the Esau fresco, but one who has a keener feeling for reality and a far deeper sense of the dramatic situation.

We will now turn to the historical evidence. The earliest and best is that of Ghiberti (early fifteenth century), who tells us simply that Giotto painted the S. Francis legend. Vasari says that Cimabue worked first in the lower church with Greek artists, and then did the whole of the upper church, except the S. Francis legend, which he ascribes to Giotto. In addition to these we have a sixteenth-century MS. and an account of the church by Petrus Rudolphus of the same period, which agree that both Giotto and Cimabue painted in the upper church.

We may take it, then, that we have fairly good evidence for ascribing the S. Francis series in the main to Giotto, and a consensus of traditional opinion that somewhere in the other frescoes we ought to discover Cimabue.

The name of Cimabue is fraught with tender associations. To the last generation, happy in its innocence, it was familiar as a household word. Browning could sing without a qualm: "My painter—who, but Cimabue?" The cult of Cimabue became fashionable; it offended Philistine nostrils and received its due castigation from Mr. Punch. And now, alas, he would be a bold man who dared to say that he admired Cimabue, who dared to do more than profess a pious belief in his existence. Only recently a distinguished critic[1] has endeavoured to hand over to Duccio di Buoninsegna the very stronghold of the Cimabue faith, the altar-piece of the Rucellai Chapel in Sta. Maria Novella. But the myth dies hard, and Florentine guides will still point out the portraits of all Cimabue's relations in the little figures round the frame. Ever since the time of Rumohr, however, who considered him to be little more than an emanation of Vasari's brain heated

[1] Dr. J. P. Richter: "Lectures on the National Gallery."

by patriotic fervour, it has been established that we
have no documentary evidence for any single picture
by him. We do know, however, that at the very end
of his life he executed the mosaic of the apse in the
cathedral at Pisa. But this is a much-restored work,
and originally can have been little but an adaptation
of a Byzantine design, and it throws no light on his
work as a painter. In any case, all criticisms of
his reputation in his own day, whether deserved or not,
must fall to the ground before Dante's celebrated lines,
"Credette Cimabue nella pittura Tener lo campo, ed
ora ha Giotto il grido," for on this point Dante is
first-rate evidence. And that being the case, there is
a probability, almost amounting to certainty, that
the man who "held the field" in painting would be
requisitioned for the greatest national undertaking of
his day, the decoration of S. Francesco at Assisi, even
though, as we have seen, it would be impossible to
accept Vasari's statement that he did the whole.

In looking for Cimabue among the groups of the
upper church which we have selected, it will be worth
while to take as an experimental guide other works
ascribed traditionally to our artist. If these should
agree in their artistic qualities with one another and
with any one group at Assisi, we shall have some probability in favour of our view. And the result of such
a process is to find in the master of the Crucifixion
our elusive and celebrated painter.

It would be wearisome to go in detail through all
these works; it will suffice to say that in certain marked
peculiarities they all agree with one another and with
the Crucifixion. The most striking likeness will be
found between the heads which appear under the
Virgin's throne in the picture in the Academy at
Florence, which Vasari attributes to Cimabue, and
the grotesque heads to the right of the Crucifixion.
There is the same crude attempt at realism, the same

peculiar matted hair, the same curious drawing of the
eye-socket which gives the appearance of spectacles.
The characteristics of this picture will again be found
in the Cimabue of the Louvre which comes from Pisa,
where he is known to have worked. Very similar, too,
in innumerable details of architectural setting, of movement of hands and heads, and of drapery is the fresco
of the Madonna Enthroned and S. Francis, in the
lower church at Assisi. Finally, the Rucellai Madonna,
in spite of its very superior qualities, which must be
due to its being a later work, answers in many detailed
tests to the characteristics of this group of paintings.[1]

And now, having found our Cimabue in the master
of the Crucifixion, what must our verdict be on his
character as an artist? Frankly we must admit that

[1] One picture, however, ascribed by Vasari to Cimabue, namely,
the Madonna of the National Gallery, does not bear the characteristics of this group. Dr. Richter's argument for giving the
Rucellai painting to Duccio depends largely on the likeness of
this to the Maesta, but there is no reason to cling so closely to
Vasari's attributions. If we except the National Gallery Madonna,
which shows the characteristics of the Siennese school, these
pictures, including the Rucellai Madonna, will be found to cohere
by many common peculiarities not shared by Duccio. Among
these we may notice the following: The eye has the upper eyelid
strongly marked; it has a peculiar languishing expression, due
in part to the large elliptical iris (Duccio's eyes have a small,
bright, round iris with a keen expression); the nose is distinctly
articulated into three segments; the mouth is generally slewed
round from the perpendicular; the hands are curiously curved
and in all the Madonnas clutch the supports of the throne; the
hair bows seen upon the halos have a constant and quite peculiar
shape; the drapery is designed in rectilinear triangular folds,
very different from Duccio's more sinuous and flowing line. The
folds of the drapery where they come to the contour of the figure
have no effect upon the form of the outline, an error which Duccio
never makes. Finally, the thrones in all these pictures have a
constant form; they are made of turned wood with a high foot-
stool, and are seen from the side; Duccio's is of stone and seen
from the front. That the Rucellai Madonna has a morbidezza
which is wanting in the earlier works can hardly be considered
a sufficient distinction to set against the formal characteristics.
It is clearly a later work, painted probably about the year 1300,
and Cimabue, like all the other artists of the time, was striving
constantly in the direction of greater fusion of tones.

he is not to be thought of in the same category with
the master of the Esau fresco, much less with Duccio
or Giotto.[1] There is, however, in his work that spark
of vitality which the Italians rightly prized above
Byzantine accomplishment. He gave to his historical
compositions a rude dramatic vigour, and to his
Madonnas and Angels a suggestion of sentimental
charm which borders on affectation; he was, in fact,
a sentimental realist whose relation to the Byzantine
masters must have been something like that of Caravaggio to the academic school of the Caracci.

We come next to the master of the Deception of
Isaac, and the closely allied, if not identical, painter
who did the Four Doctors of the vault. We have
already noticed the likeness of these works to the
legend of S. Francis, which we may take provisionally
to be Giotto's; but, in spite of the similarity of technique, they are inspired by a very diverse sentiment.
They are not dramatic and intense as Giotto's; they
show a more conscious aspiration after style; the
artist will not allow the requirements of formal beauty
to be disturbed by the desire for expressive and life-
like gestures. Where, then, could an artist of this
period acquire such a sense of pure classic beauty in
painting? In sculpture it might be possible to find
classic models throughout Italy as Niccolò did at Pisa,
but Rome was the only place which could fulfil the
requirements for a painter. There must at this time
have been many more remains of classical painting

[1] I should speak now both with greater confidence and much
greater enthusiasm of Cimabue. The attempt of certain scholars
to dispose of him as a myth has broken down. The late Mr. H. P.
Horne found that the documents cited by Dr. Richter to prove
that Duccio executed the Rucellai Madonna referred to another
picture. I had also failed in my estimate to consider fully the
superb crucifix by Cimabue in the Museum of Sta. Croce, a work
of supreme artistic merit. In general my defence of Cimabue,
though right enough as far as it goes, appears to me too timid
and my estimate of his artistic quality far too low (1920).

among the ruins of the Palatine than are now to be seen, and it is a natural conclusion that the artist who painted the figure of Rachel was directly inspired by them. Nor is there anything difficult in the assumption that this unknown precursor of Giotto was a Roman artist, for the Roman school of painting was by far the most precocious of any in Italy. At Subiaco there are frescoes, some of which must date from the lifetime of S. Francis, which already, as in the portrait of S. Francis himself, show a certain freedom from Byzantine formalism. But it is in the works of the Cosmati, Jacopo Torriti, Rusutti, and Cavallini in the latter half of the thirteenth century that we see how vigorous and progressive an art was springing up in Rome.[1] Had not the removal of the Popes to Avignon in the fourteenth century left the city a prey to internal discord, we can hardly doubt that the Roman would have been one of the greatest and earliest developed schools of Italian painting. As it is, we find in the mosaics under the apse of Sta. Maria in Trastevere, executed about the year 1290, compositions in every way comparable to Giotto's frescoes. These mosaics, too, have architectural accessories which are very similar to the architecture of the "Doctors of the Church" at Assisi. The architecture based on a study of classic forms is of the kind always associated with the Cosmati family. It will be seen that it is quite distinct from the architecture of Cimabue's and Duccio's Madonnas, but that it becomes the normal treatment in Giotto's frescoes.

There is, then, a curiously close analogy between the origins of neo-Christian painting and neo-Christian sculpture in Italy; just as Giovanni Pisano's work was preceded by the purely classic revival which culminated in Niccolò's Baptistery pulpit, so in painting Giotto's

---

[1] The important position here assigned to the Roman school has been confirmed by the subsequent discovery of Cavallini's frescoes in Sta. Cecilia at Rome (1920).

work emerges from a similar classic revival based on the study of Roman wall-paintings. The perfect similarity between Niccolò Pisano's sentiment and that of the master of the Esau fresco may be realised by comparing the action of Rachel's hand in the fresco with that of the Virgin in the Annunciation of the Baptistery pulpit. In both we have the same autarchic conception of character conveyed by the same measured ease of gesture, which contrasts vividly with the more expansive ideals of neo-Christian art, of which Giotto appears from the first as the most perfect representative.

In examining the series of frescoes describing the life of S. Francis we find varieties in the proportions of the figures and in the types of features which suggest the co-operation of more than one artist, but the spirit that inspires the compositions throughout is one. And this afflatus which suddenly quickens so much that was either tentative or narrowly accomplished into a new fulness of life, a new richness of expression, is, we may feel certain, due to the genius of Giotto.

If we look at one of these frescoes, such, for example, as the Presepio at Greccio, and at the same time, endeavour to transport ourselves into the position of a contemporary spectator, what will strike us most immediately and make the most startling general impression is its actuality. Here at last after so many centuries of copying the traditional forms handed down from a moribund Pagan art—centuries during which these abstractions had become entirely divorced from the life of the time—here at last was an artist who gave a scene as it must have happened, with every circumstance evidently and literally rendered. The scene of the institution of the Presepio takes place in a little chapel divided from the body of the church by a marble wall. The pulpit and crucifix are therefore seen from behind, the latter leaning forward into the church and showing from the chapel only the wooden battens and fastenings of the back. The singing-desk in the centre is drawn with every detail of screws and adjustments, while the costume of the bystanders is merely the ordinary fashionable dress of the day. The research for actuality could not be carried farther than this. When some years ago a French painter painted the scene of Christ at the house of the Pharisee with the figures in evening dress it aroused the most vehement protests, and produced for a time a shock of bewilderment and surprise. This is not to suggest any real analogy between the works of the two artists, but merely that the innovation made by Giotto must have been in every way as surprising to his contemporaries. Nor was Giotto's, like M. Beraud's, a *succès de scandale*; on the contrary, it was immediately recognised as satisfying a want which had been felt ever since the legend of S. Francis, the setting of which belonged to their own time and country, had been incorporated by the Italians in their mythology. The earliest artists had tried to treat the subject according to the formulæ of Byzantine biblical scenes, but with such unsatisfactory results as may be seen in the altar-piece of the Bardi Chapel of Sta. Croce at Florence. In Giotto's frescoes at Assisi it acquired for the first time a treatment in which the desire for actuality was fully recognised. But actuality alone would not have satisfied Giotto's patrons; it was necessary that the events should be presented as scenes of everyday life, but it was also necessary that they should possess that quality of universal and eternal significance which distinguishes a myth from a mere historical event. It was even more necessary that they should be heroic than that they should be actual. And it was in his power to satisfy such apparently self-contradictory conditions that Giotto's unique genius manifested itself. It was this that made him the greatest story-teller in line, the supreme epic-painter of the world. The reconcilia-

tion of these two aims, actuality and universality,
is indeed the severest strain on the power of expression.
To what a temperature must the imagination be raised
before it can fuse in its crucible those refractory squalid
trivialities unconsecrated by time and untinged by
romance with which the artist must deal if he is to
be at once "topical" and heroic, to be at one and
the same time in "Ercles' vein" and Mrs. Gamp's.
Even in literature it is a rare feat. Homer could accomplish it, and Dante, but most poets must find a way
round. In Dante the power is constantly felt. He
could not only introduce the politics and personalities
of his own time, but he could use such similes as that
of old tailors peering for their needles' eyes, a half-
burnt piece of paper, dogs nozzling for fleas, and still
more unsavoury trivialities, without for a moment
owering the high key in which his comedy was pitched.
The poet deals, however, with the vague and blurred
mental images which words call up, but the painter must
actually present the semblance of the thing in all its drab
familiarity. And yet Giotto succeeded. He could make
the local and particular stand for a universal idea.

But, without detracting in any way from what was
due to Giotto's superlative genius, it may be admitted
that something was given by the propitious moment
of his advent. For the optics of the imagination are
variable: in an age like the present, men and events
grow larger as they recede into the mist of the past;
it is rarely that we think of a man as truly great till
he has for long received the consecration of death.
But there must be periods when men have a surer
confidence in their own judgments—periods of such
creative activity that men can dare to measure the
reputations of their contemporaries, which are of their
own creation, against the reputations of antiquity—
and in such periods the magnifying, mythopoetical
effect, which for us comes only with time, takes place

at once, and swells their contemporaries to heroic proportions. It was thus that Dante saw those of his own time—could even see himself—in the proportions they must always bear. The fact that S. Francis was canonised two years after his death, and within twenty years was commemorated by the grandest monument in Italy, is a striking proof of that superb self-confidence.

We will return to the frescoes: the evidence for their being in the main by Giotto himself rests not only on the general consensus of tradition, but upon the technical characteristics and, most of all, upon the imaginative conception of the subjects. None the less, in so big a work it is probable that assistants were employed to carry out Giotto's designs, and this will account for many slight discrepancies of style. Certain frescoes, however—notably the last three of the series—show such marked differences that we must suppose that one of these assistants rose to the level of an original creative artist.

In the fresco of S. Francis kneeling before the Pope, we have already noticed Giotto's close connection with the artists of the Roman school. Their influence is not confined to the figures and drapery; the architecture—in which it may be noted, by the way, that Giotto has already arrived instinctively at the main ideas of linear perspective—with its minute geometrical inlays, its brackets and mouldings, derived from classical forms, is entirely in the manner of the Cosmati. But the composition illustrates, none the less, the differences which separate him from the master of the Esua fresco. Giotto is at this stage of his career not only less accomplished, but he has nothing of that painter's elegant classical grace. He has, instead, the greatest and rarest gift of dramatic expressiveness. For though the poses, especially of the bishop seated on the Pope's left, lack grace, and the faces show but little research for positive beauty or regularity of feature, the actual

scene, the dramatic situation, is given in an entirely
new and surprising way. Of what overwhelming importance for the history of the world this situation
was, perhaps Giotto himself could scarcely realise.
For this probably represents, not the approbation of
the order of minor brethren by Honorius III., which
was a foregone conclusion, but the permission to
preach given by Innocent III., a far more critical moment
in the history of the movement. For Innocent III.,
in whom the Papacy reached the zenith of its power,
had already begun the iniquitous Albigensian crusade,
and was likely to be suspicious of any unofficial religious
teaching. It cannot have been with unmixed pleasure
that he saw before him this poverty-stricken group
of Francis and his eleven followers, whose appearance
declared in the plainest terms their belief in that primitive communistic Christianity which, in the case of
Petrus Waldus, had been branded by excommunication.
In fact, the man who now asked for the Papal blessing
on his mission was in most respects a Waldensian.
Francis—the name Francesco is itself significant—
was probably by birth, certainly by predilection[1] and
temperament, half a Frenchman; his mother came from
Provence, and his father had business connections at
Lyons; so that it is not impossible that Francis was
influenced by what he knew, through them, of the
Waldensian movement. In any case, his teaching was
nearly identical with that of Petrus Waldus; both taught
religious individualism and, by precept at all events,
communism. It was, therefore, not unnatural that

[1] "Drunken with the love of compassion of Christ, the blessed
Francis would at times do such-like things as this: for the passing
sweet melody of the spirit within him, seething over outwardly,
did often find utterance in the French tongue, and the strain of
the divine whisper that his ear had caught would break forth
into a French song of joyous exulting." Then pretending with
two sticks to play a viol, "and making befitting gestures, (he)
would sing in French of our Lord Jesus Christ."—"The Mirror
of perfection," edited by P. Sabatier, transl. by S. Evans.

Innocent should not respond at once to S. Francis'
application. According to one legend, the Pope's first
advice to him was to consort with swine, as befitted
one of his miserable appearance. But, whatever his
spontaneous impulses may have been, he had the
good sense to accept the one man through whom
the Church could again become popular and
democratic.

Of all that this acceptance involved, no one who
lived before the Reformation could understand the
full significance, but Giotto has here expressed something of the dramatic contrasts involved in this meeting
of the greatest of saints and the most dominating of
popes—something of the importance of the moment
when the great heretic was recognised by the Church.

In the fresco of S. Francis before the Sultan we
have a means of comparing Giotto at this period
with the later Giotto of the Bardi Chapel, in Florence,
where the same scene is treated with more intimate
psychological imagination; but here already the story
is told with a vividness and simplicity which none
but Giotto could command. The weak and sinuous
curves of the discomfited sages, the ponderous and
massive contour of the indignant Sultan, show that
Giotto's command of the direct symbolism of line
is at least as great as Duccio's in the Three Maries,
while his sense of the roundness and solid relief of the
form is, as Mr. Berenson[1] has ably pointed out, far
greater. We find in the Sultan, indeed, the type for which
Giotto showed a constant, predilection—a well-formed,
massive body, with high rounded shoulders and short
neck, but with small and shapely hands. As is natural
in the work of an artist who set himself so definitely
to externalise the tension of a critical moment, his
hands are always eloquent; it is impossible to find

[1] "Florentine Painters of the Renaissance and Central Italian
Painters of the Renaissance," by B. Berenson.

in his work a case where the gestures of the hands
are not explicit indications of a particular emotion.
The architecture in this fresco is a remarkable evidence
of the classical tendencies which he inherited from the
Cosmati school. The Sultan's throne has, it is true,
a quasi-Gothic gable, but the coffered soffit, and the
whole of the canopy opposite to it, with its winged
genii, pilasters, and garlands are derived from classic
sources.

We have already considered the Presepio as an
example of Giotto's power of giving the actual setting
of a scene without losing its heroic quality. It is also
an example of his power of visualising the psychological
situation; here, the sudden thrill which permeates an
assembly at a moment of unwonted exaltation. It
depicts the first representation of the Nativity instituted
at Greccio by S. Francis; it is the moment at which
he takes the image of the Infant Christ in his arms,
when, to the ecstatic imaginations of the bystanders,
it appeared for an instant transformed into a living
child of transcendent beauty. The monks at the back
are still singing the Lauds (one can almost tell what
note each is singing, so perfect is Giotto's command
of facial expression), but the immediate bystanders
and the priest are lost in wrapt contemplation of S.
Francis and the Child.[1]

One of the most beautiful of the whole series is
the fresco which represents the nuns of S. Clare
meeting the Saint's body as it is borne to burial.
Throughout the series Giotto took Bonaventura's
Life as his text and it is interesting to see how near
akin the two renderings are, both alike inspired by
that new humanity of feeling which S. Francis' life

[1] This was the first "representation" of the kind in Italy, and
is of interest as being the beginning of the Italian Drama, and
also of that infinite series of allegorical pageants, sometimes
sacred, sometimes secular, which for three centuries played such
a prominent part in city life and affected Italian art very intimately.

E

had aroused. Having described the beauty of the Saint's dead body,

of which the limbs were so soft and delicate to the touch that they seemed to have returned to the tenderness of a child's, and appeared by manifest signs to be innocent as never having done wrong, so like a child's were they,

he adds,

Therefore it is not to be marvelled at if seeing a body so white and seeing therein those black nails and that wound in the side which seemed to be a fresh red rose of spring, if those that saw it felt therefor great wonder and joy. And in the morning when it was day the companies and people of the city and all the country round came together, and being instructed to translate that most holy body from that place to the city of Assisi, moved with great solemnity of hymns and songs and divine offices, and with a multitude of torches and of candles lighted and with branches of trees in their hands; and with such solemnity going towards the city of Assisi and passing by the church of S. Damiano, in which stayed Clara the noble virgin who is to-day a saint on earth and in heaven, they rested there a little. She and her holy virgins were comforted to see and kiss that most holy body of their father the blessed Francis adorned with those holy stigmata and white and shining as has been said.

Bonaventura, we see, had already conceived the scene with such consummate artistic skill that it was, as it were, ready made for Giotto. He had only to translate that description into line and colour; and in doing so he has lost nothing of its beauty. Giotto, like Bonaventura, is apparently perfectly simple, perfectly direct and literal, and yet the result is in both cases a work of the rarest imaginative power. Nor is it easy to analyze its mysterious charm. Giotto was a great painter in the strictest and most technical sense of the word, but his technical perfection is not easily appreciated in these damaged works and one cannot explain the effect this produces by any actual beauty

of the surface quality of the painting; it depends rather
on our perception, through the general disposition
and action of the figures, of Giotto's attitude to life,
of the instinctive rightness of feeling through which
he was enabled to visualise the scene in its simplest
and most inevitable form.

We come now to the last three frescoes of the series
which show such marked differences from the rest,
though some of the peculiarities, the minute hands and
elegant features, appear in parts of some of the preceding frescoes, notably in our last: we may imagine
that an assistant working under Giotto was, as the
work progressed, given a larger and larger share in the
execution, and finally carried out the last three frescoes
alone. But this is pure hypothesis; all we can do at
present is to note the difference not only of types, but
even to some extent in the manner of conception, that
they evince. One of them recounts the story of a woman
of Benevento devoted to S. Francis, who died after
forgetting one of her sins in her last confession. At
the intercession of the dead Saint she was allowed to
come to life again, finish her confession, and so defeat
of his prey the black devil who had already come for
her soul. Here the whole spacing out of the composition
indicates a peculiar feeling, very different from Giotto's.
The artist crowds his figures into narrow, closely-
packed groups, and leaves vast spaces of bare wall
between. In this particular instance the result is very
impressive; it intensifies the supreme importance
of the confession and emphasises the loneliness and
isolation of the soul that has already once passed away.
When we look at the individual figures the differences
are even more striking; the long thin figures, the repetition of perpendicular lines, the want of variety in the
poses of the heads, a certain timidity in the movements,
the long masks, too big in proportion for the heads,
the tiny elegant features, elongated necks, and minute

hands—all these characteristics contrast with Giotto's tendency to massive proportions and easy expansive movements. Not that these figures have not great beauty; only it is of a recondite and exquisite kind. The artist that created these types must have loved what was sought out and precious; though living so long before Raphael, he must have been something of a "pre-Raphaelite."

We have no clue to the identity of this pseudo-Giotto; he is quite distinct from Giotto's known pupils, and indeed may rather have been a contemporary artist who came under Giotto's influence than one trained by him. Besides the frescoes at Assisi, we are fortunate enough to possess one other picture by this interesting artist. It is a small altar-piece dedicated to S. Cecilia, which hangs in the corridor of the Uffizi, and has been attributed both to Cimabue and to Giotto. The long Rossetti-like necks and heads, the poses, in which elegance is preferred to expressiveness, and the concentration of the figures so as to leave large empty spaces even in these small compositions, are sufficient grounds for attributing it to Giotto's fellow-worker at Assisi.[1]

In the year 1298 Giotto entered into a contract with Cardinal Stefaneschi to execute for him the mosaic of the "Navicella," now in the porch of S. Peter's. We have in this the first ascertainable date of Giotto's life. It is one which, however, fits very well with the internal evidences of his style, as it would give the greater part of the last decade of the thirteenth century as the period of Giotto's activity in the Upper Church of Assisi. One other work on

[1] The Master of the Cecilia altar-piece has been the object of much research since this article was written, and a considerable number of important works are now ascribed to him with some confidence. He has been tentatively identified with Buffalmacco by Dr Siren. See *Burl. Mag.*, December, 1919; January, October, 1920.

the evidence of style we may attribute to the master's pre-Roman period, and that is the Madonna of the Academy at Florence. Here Giotto followed the lines of Cimabue's enthroned Madonnas, though with his own greatly increased sense of solidity in the modelling and vivacity in the poses. It cannot, however, be considered as a prepossessing work. It may be due to restoration that the picture shows no signs of Giotto's peculiar feeling for tonality; but even the design is scarcely satisfactory, the relation of the Madonna to the throne is such that her massive proportions leave an impression of ungainliness rather than of grandeur. In the throne itself he has made an experiment in the new Gothic architecture, but he has hardly managed to harmonise it with the earlier classic forms of the Cosmati, which still govern the main design. We shall see that in his work at Rome he overcame all these difficulties.

In Rome Giotto worked chiefly for Cardinal Stefaneschi. This is significant of Giotto's close relations with the Roman school, for it was Bartolo, another member of the same family, who commissioned the remarkable mosaics of Sta. Maria in Trastevere, executed in 1290, mosaics which show how far the Roman school had already advanced towards the new art, of which Giotto's work was the consummation.

The mosaic of the "Navicella," which was the greatest undertaking of Giotto's activity in Rome, is unfortunately terribly restored. We can, however, still recognise the astonishing dramatic force of the conception and the unique power which Giotto possessed of giving a vivid presentation of a particular event, accompanied by the most circumstantial details, and at the same time suggesting to the imagination a symbolical interpretation of universal and abstract significance. Even the surprising intrusion of a *genre*

motive in the fisherman peacefully angling on the shore
does not disturb our recognition of this universal interpretation, which puts so clearly the relation of the
ship of the Church, drifting helplessly with its distraught
crew, to the despairing Peter, who has here the character
of an emissary and intermediary, and the impassive
and unapproachable figure of Christ himself.

The daring originality which Giotto shows in placing
the predominant figure at the extreme edge of the
composition, the feeling for perspective which enabled
him to give verisimilitude to the scene by throwing
back the ship into the middle distance, the new freedom
and variety in the movements of the Apostles in the
boat, by which the monotony of the eleven figures
crowded into so limited a space is avoided, are proofs
of Giotto's rare power of invention, a power which
enabled him to treat even the most difficult abstractions
with the same vivid sense of reality as the dramatic
incidents of contemporary life. It is not to be wondered
at that this should be the work most frequently
mentioned by the Italian writers of the Renaissance.
The storm-gods blowing their Triton's horns are a
striking instance of how much Giotto assimilated at
this time from Pagan art.

But of far greater beauty are the panels for the
high altar of S. Peter's, also painted for Cardinal
Stefaneschi, and now to be seen in the sacristy, where
the more obvious beauties of Melozzo da Forli's music-
making angels too often lead to their being overlooked.
And yet, unnoticed in the dark corners of the room,
they have escaped the attentions of restorers and glow
with all the rare translucency of Giotto's tempera.

These are the first pictures we have examined by
Giotto in which we are able to appreciate at all the
beauty and subtlety of his tone contrasts, for not only
have the frescoes of the upper church at Assisi and
the "Madonna" of the Academy suffered severely

from restoration, but it is probable that in his youthful
works he had not freed himself altogether from the
harsher tonality of earlier art. Here, however, Giotto
shows that power which is distinctive of the greatest
masters of paint, of developing a form within a strictly
limited scale of tone, drawing out of the slightest
contrasts their fullest expressiveness for the rendering
of form; a method which, though adopted from an
intuitive feeling for pure beauty, gives a result which
can only be described as that of an enveloping atmosphere surrounding the forms.[1]

The kneeling figure, presumably Cardinal Stefaneschi
himself, in the "Christ enthroned" is an admirable
instance of this quality. With what tender, scarcely
perceptible gradations, with what a limited range from
dark to light is the figure expressed! and yet it is not
flat, the form is perfectly realised between the two
sweeping curves whose simplicity would seem, but for
the masterly modelling, to prevent the possibility of
their containing a human figure. The portrait is as
remarkable in sentiment as in execution. The very
conception of introducing a donor into such a composition was new.[2] It was a sign of the new individualism
which marked the whole of the great period of Italian
art, and finally developed into extravagance. The
donor having once found his way into pictures of
sacred ceremonial remained, but he not infrequently
found it difficult to comport himself becomingly amid
celestial surroundings; as he became more important,
and heaven itself became less so, he asserted himself
with unseemly self-assurance, until at last his matter-
of-fact countenance, rendered with prosaic fidelity,

[1] This quality is to be distinguished from that conscious
naturalistic study of atmospheric envelopment which engrossed
the attention of some artists of the cinquecento; it is a decorative
quality which may occur at any period in the development of painting if only an artist arises gifted with a sufficiently delicate sensitive-
ness to the surface-quality of his work.

[2] I cannot recall any example in pre-Giottesque art.

stares out at the spectator in contemptuous indifference to the main action of the composition, the illusion of which it effectually destroys.

But here, where the idea is new, it has no such jarring effect; it is not yet a stereotyped formula, an excuse for self-advertisement or social display, but the direct outcome of a poetical and pious thought; and Giotto, with his unique rightness of feeling, has expressed, by the hand clinging to the throne and the slightly bent head, just the appropriate attitude of humble adoration, which he contrasts with the almost nonchalant ease and confidence of the angels. Even in so purely cere-monial a composition as this Giotto contrives to create a human situation.

In the planning of this picture Giotto has surpassed not only Duccio's and Cimabue's versions of the Enthronement motive but his own earlier work at Florence. The throne, similar in construction to that in the Academy picture, no longer shows the incon-sistencies of two conflicting styles, but is of pure and exquisitely proportioned Gothic; the difficult perspective of the arches at the side is rendered with extraordinary skill though without mathematical accuracy. The relation of the figure of Christ to the throne is here entirely satisfactory, with the result that the great size of the figure no longer appears unnatural, but as an easily accepted symbol of divinity. In the drawing of the face of the Christ he has retained the hieratic solemnity given by the rigid delineation of Byzantine art.

But if the "Christ enthroned" is a triumph of well-calculated proportions, the "Crucifixion of S. Peter" which formed one side of the triptych, is even more remarkable for the beauty of its spacing and the ingenuity of its arrangement.

In designing such a panel with its narrow cusped arch and gold background, the artist's first considera-tion must be its effect as mere pattern when seen on the altar at the end of a church. In his frescoes, Giotto's first preoccupation was with the drama to be presented; here it was with the effect of sumptuous pattern.

And the given data out of which the pattern was to be made were by no means tractable. The subject of the Crucifixion of S. Peter was naturally not a favourite one with artists, and scarcely any succeeded in it entirely, even in the small dimensions of a predella piece, to which it was generally relegated. For it is almost impossible to do away with the unpleasant effect of a figure seen thus upside down. The outstretched arms, which in the crucifixion of Christ give a counterbalancing line to the long horizontal of the spectators, here only increase the difficulty of the single upright. But Giotto, by a brilliant inspiration,[1] found his solution in the other fact given by his subject —namely, that the martyrdom took place between the goals of the Circus of Nero. By making these huge pyramids adapted from two well-known Roman monuments—the Septizonium and the pyramid of Cestius —he has obtained from the gold background just that dignified effect of spreading out above and contracting below which is so effective in renderings of the crucifixion of Christ, an effect which he still further emphasises by the two angels, whose spreading wings and floating draperies increase the brocade-like richness of the symmetrical pattern.

Nor, the pattern once assured, has Giotto failed of vivid dramatic presentation. It is surprising to find crowded into so small a space so many new poses all beautifully expressive of the individual shades of a common feeling; the woman to the left of the cross leaning her head on her hand as though sorrow had become a physical pain: the beautiful figure of the youth, with long waving hair, who throws back both

---

[1] Derived, no doubt, but greatly modified, from Cimabue's treatment of the subject at Assisi.

arms with a despairing gesture; the woman lifting
her robe to wipe her tears; and, most exquisite of all,
and most surprising, in its novelty and truth to life,
the figure of the girl to the left, drawn towards the
terrible scene by a motion of sympathy and yet shrink-
ing back with instinctive shyness and terror. In the
child alone Giotto has, as was usually the case, failed
of a rhythmical and expressive pose. And what an
entirely new study of life is seen here in the variety
of the types! In one—the man whose profile cuts
the sky to the left—he seems to have been indebted
to some Roman portrait-bust; another, on horseback
to the left, is clearly a Mongolian type, with slant
eyes and pigtail, a curious proof of the intercourse
with the extreme East which the Franciscan missionaries
had already established. In the drawing of the nude
figure of S. Peter, in spite of the unfortunate proportion
of the head, the same direct study of nature has enabled
Giotto to realise the structure of the figure more
adequately than any artist since Roman times. One
can well understand the astonishment and delight
of Giotto's contemporaries at this unfolding of the
new possibilities of art, which could now interpret
all the variety and richness of human life and could
so intensify its appeal to the emotions. One other
peculiarity of this picture is interesting and characteristic of Giotto's attitude. In painting the frame of his
panel he did not merely add figures as decorative and
symbolic accessories, he brought them into relation
with the central action, for each of them gazes at S.
Peter with a different expression of pity and grief.
Giotto had to be dramatic even in his frames.[1]

That Giotto remained in Rome till after the great
Jubilee of 1300 is shown by the fragment of his fresco

[1] The attribution of the Stefaneschi altar-piece to Giotto is
much disputed and some authorities give it to Bernardo Daddi.
I still incline to the idea that it is the work of Giotto and the starting
point of Bernardo Daddi's style (1920).

of the Papal Benediction which still remains on a pillar of S. John Lateran. There is every probability that at this time he met Dante, who was collecting the materials for the terrible portrait of Boniface VIII. which he drew in the "Inferno."

The next ascertainable date in Giotto's life is that of the decoration of the Arena chapel at Padua, begun in 1305. Here at last we are on indisputable ground. The decoration of this chapel was conceived by Giotto as a single whole, and was entirely carried out by him, though doubtless with the help of assistants, and although it has suffered from restoration it remains the completest monument to his genius. The general effect of these ample silhouettes of golden yellow and red on a ground of clear ultramarine is extraordinarily harmonious, and almost gay. But essentially the design is made up of the sum of a number of separate compositions. The time had not come for co-ordinating these into a single scheme, as Michelangelo did in the ceiling of the Sistine. In the composition of the separate scenes Giotto here shows for the first time his full powers. Nearly every one of these is an entirely original discovery of new possibilities in the relation of forms to one another. The contours of the figures evoke to the utmost the ideal comprehension of volume and mass. The space in which the figures move is treated almost as in a bas-relief, of which they occupy a preponderant part. As compared with the designs at Assisi the space is restricted, and the figures amplified so that the plastic unity of the whole design is more immediately apprehended. I doubt whether in any single building one can see so many astonishing discoveries of formal relations as Giotto has here made. Almost every composition gives one the shock of a discovery at once simple, inevitable, and instantly apprehended, and yet utterly unforeseeable. In most compositions one can guess at some of the steps by which the formal

relations were established. Here one is at a loss to
conceive by what flight of imagination the synthesis has
been attained. We will consider a few in greater detail.

Giotto was, I believe, the first artist to represent the
Resurrection by the *Noli me tangere*. The Byzantines
almost invariably introduced the Descent into Hades
or the Three Maries at the Tomb. In any case it is
characteristic of Giotto to choose a subject where the
human situation is so intimate and the emotions
expressed are so poignant. Here, as in the "Navicella,"
where he was free to invent a new composition, he
discards the bilateral arrangement, which was almost
invariable in Byzantine art, and concentrates all the
interest in one corner of the composition. The angels
on the tomb are damaged and distorted, but in the head
and hands of the Magdalene we can realise Giotto's
greatly increased power and delicacy of modelling
as compared with the frescoes at Assisi. It is impossible
for art to convey more intensely than this the beauty
of such a movement of impetuous yearning. The
action of the Christ is as vividly realised; almost too
obviously, indeed, does he seem to be edging out of
the composition in order to escape the Magdalene's
outstretched hands. This is a striking instance of
that power which Giotto possessed more than any
other Italian, more indeed than any other artist except
Rembrandt, the power of making perceptible the flash
of mutual recognition which passes between two souls
at a moment of sudden illumination.

In the "Pieta" a more epic conception is realised,
for the impression conveyed is of a universal and cosmic
disaster: the air is rent with the shrieks of desperate
angels whose bodies are contorted in a raging frenzy
of compassion. And the effect is due in part to the
increased command, which the Paduan frescoes show,
of simplicity and logical directness of design. These
massive boulderlike forms, these draperies cut by only

a few large sweeping folds, which suffice to give the
general movement of the figure with unerring precision,
all show this new tendency in Giotto's art as compared
with the more varied detail, the more individual
characterisation, of his early works. It is by this
consciously acquired and masterly simplicity that
Giotto keeps here, in spite of the unrestrained extravagance of passion, the consoling dignity of style. If
one compares it, for example, with the works of Flemish
painters, who explored the depths of human emotion
with a similar penetrating and sympathetic curiosity,
one realises the importance of what all the great Italians
inherited from Græco-Roman civilisation—the urbanity
of a great style. And nowhere is it felt more than here,
where Giotto is dealing with emotions which classical
art scarcely touched.

It is interesting that Giotto should first have attained
to this perfect understanding of style at Padua, where
he was, as we know, in constant intercourse with Dante.
Dante must have often watched him, perhaps helped
him by suggestions, in decorating the chapel built
with the ill-gotten wealth of that Scrovegni whom he
afterwards seated amid the usurers on the burning
sands of Hell.

It is mainly by means of the composition and the
general conception of pose and movement that Giotto
expresses the dramatic idea. And regarded from that
point of view, these frescoes are an astounding proof
of Giotto's infallible intuitions. The characters he has
created here are as convincing, as ineffaceable, as any
that have been created by poets. The sad figure of
Joachim is one never to be forgotten. In every incident
of his sojourn in the wilderness, after the rejection of
his offering in the temple, his appearance indicates
exactly his mental condition. When he first comes to
the sheepfold, he gazes with such set melancholy on
the ground that the greeting of his dog and his shepherds

cannot arouse his attention; when he makes a sacrifice he crawls on hands and knees in the suspense of expectation, watching for a sign from heaven; even in his sleep we guess at his melancholy dreams; and in the scene where he meets his wife at the Golden Gate on his return, Giotto has touched a chord of feeling at least as profound as can be reached by the most consummate master of the art of words.

It is true that in speaking of these one is led inevitably to talk of elements in the work which modern criticism is apt to regard as lying outside the domain of pictorial art. It is customary to dismiss all that concerns the dramatic presentation of the subject as literature or illustration, which is to be sharply distinguished from the qualities of design. But can this clear distinction be drawn in fact? The imaginings of a playwright, a dramatic poet, and a dramatic painter have much in common, but they are never at any point identical. Let us suppose a story to be treated by all three: to each, as he dwells on the legend, the imagination will present a succession of images, but those images, even at their first formation, will be quite different in each case, they will be conditioned and coloured by the art which the creator practises, by his past observation of nature with a view to presentment in that particular art. The painter, like Giotto, therefore, actually imagines in terms of figures capable of pictorial presentment, he does not merely translate a poetically dramatic vision into pictorial terms. And to be able to do this implies a constant observation of natural forms with a bias towards the discovery of pictorial beauty. To be able then, to conceive just the appropriate pose of a hand to express the right idea of character and emotion in a picture, is surely as much a matter of a painter's vision as to appreciate the relative "values" of a tree and cloud so as to convey the mood proper to a particular landscape.

Before leaving the Paduan frescoes, I must allude to those allegorical figures of the virtues and vices in which Giotto has, as it were, distilled the essence of his understanding of human nature. These personified virtues and vices were the rhetorical commonplaces of the day, but Giotto's intuitive understanding of the expression of emotion enabled him to give them a profound significance. He has in some succeeded in giving not merely a person under the influence of a given passion, but the abstract passion itself, not merely an angry woman, but anger. To conceive thus a figure possessed absolutely by a single passion implied an excursion beyond the regions of experience; no merely scientific observation of the effects of emotion would have enabled him to conceive the figure of Anger. It required an imagination that could range the remotest spaces thus to condense in visible form the bestial madness of the passion, to depict what Blake would have called the "diabolical abstract" of anger.

We come now to the last great series of frescoes by Giotto which we possess, those of the Bardi and Peruzzi chapels of Sta. Croce, his maturest and most consummate works. From the very first Giotto had to the full the power of seizing upon whatever in the forms of nature expressed life and emotion, but the perfect understanding of the conditions of a suave and gracious style was only slowly acquired. In the Florentine frescoes it is the geniality, the persuasiveness of the style which first strikes us. They have, indeed, an almost academic perfection of design.

The comparison of the "Death of S. Francis" here with the early fresco of the subject at Assisi shows how far Giotto has moved from the literal realism of his first works. At Assisi crowds of people push round the bier, soldiers and citizens come in to see, there is all the shifting variety of the actual event. Here the composition is sublimated and refined, reduced to its purest elements. The scene is still vividly, intensely real, but it is apprehended in a more pensive and meditative vein. There is in the composition a feeling for space which imposes a new mood of placidity and repose. This composition became the typical formula for such subjects throughout the Renaissance, but it was never again equalled. In spite of its apparent ease and simplicity, it is really by the subtlest art that all these figures are grouped in such readily apprehended masses without any sense of crowding and with such variety of gesture in the figures. The fresco, which had remained for more than a century under a coat of whitewash, was discovered in 1841 and immediately disfigured by utter restoration. The artist,[1] with a vague idea that Giotto was a decorative artist, and that decoration meant something ugly and unnatural, surrounded the figures with hard inexpressive lines. We can, therefore, only guess, by our knowledge of Giotto elsewhere, and by the general idea of pose, how perfect was the characterisation of the actors in the scene, how each responded according to his temperament to the general sorrow, some in humble prostration, one with a more intimate and personal affection, and one, to whom the vision of the ascending soul is apparent, wrapt in mystic ecstasy.

An interesting characteristic of these late frescoes is the revival which they declare of Giotto's early love for classical architecture. He may well have recognised the pictorial value of the large untroubled rectangular spaces which it allowed. In the "Salome" he has approached even more nearly to purely classic forms than in his earliest frescoes at Assisi. The building has an almost Palladian effect with its square parapets surmounted by statues, some of which are clearly

[1] His name was Bianchi. 'Faut il se plaindre,' says M. Maurice Denis in his Théories, 'qu'un Bianchi, plutôt que les laisser périr, ait ajouté un peu de la froidure de Flandrin aux fresques de Giotto à Santa Croce.'

derived from the antique. In the soldier who brings in the Baptist's head he has reverted to the costume of the Roman soldier, whereas, in the allegory of Chastity, the soldiers wear mediæval winged helmets.

The fact that there is a free copy of this fresco by the Lorenzetti at Siena made in 1331 gives us the period before which this must have been finished. Here again the mood is singularly placid, but the intensity with which Giotto realised a particularly dramatic moment is shown by a curious detail in which this differs from the usual rendering of the scene. Most artists, wishing to express the essentials of the story, make Salome continue her dance while the head is brought in. But Giotto was too deep a psychologist to make such an error. At the tragic moment she stops dancing and makes sad music on her lyre, to show that she, too, is not wanting in proper sensibility.

There is evidence in these frescoes of an artistic quality which we could scarcely have believed possible, and yet, as it is most evident in those parts which are least damaged, it is impossible not to believe that Giotto possessed it; and that is the real feeling for chiaroscuro which these paintings show. It is not merely that the light falls in one direction, though even that was a conception which was scarcely grasped before Masaccio, but that Giotto actually composes by light and shade, subordinates figures or groups of figures by letting them recede into gloom and brings others into prominent light. This is particularly well seen in the "Ascension of S. John," where the shadow of the building is made use of to unify the composition and give depth and relief to the imagined space. It is also an example of that beautiful atmospheric tonality of which I have already spoken. In the figure of S. John himself, Giotto seems to have the freedom and ease which we associate with art of a much later date. There is scarcely a hint of archaism in this figure. The head, with its perfect fusion of tones, its atmospheric envelopment, seems already nearly as modern as a head by Titian. Even the colour scheme, the rich earthy reds, the intense sweet blues of the figures relieved against a broken green-grey, is a strange anticipation of Cinquecento art. It seems as though Giotto in these works had himself explored the whole of the promised land to which he led Italian painting.

It is true that we are conscious of a certain archaism here in the relations of the figures and the architecture. A certain violence is done to that demand for verisimilitude which, perhaps wrongly, we now invariably make. But in the "Raising of Drusiana," even this demand is met. Here the figures all have their just proportions to one another, and to the buildings, and to the town wall which stretches behind them. The scene is imagined, not merely according to the conditions of the dramatic idea, but according to the possibilities and limitations of actual figures moving in a three dimensional space; even the perspective of the ground is understood. Such an imaginative construction of three dimensional space had its disadvantages as well as its advantages for art, but in any case it is an astonishing indication of Giotto's genius that he thus foresaw the conditions which in the end would be accepted universally in European art. There is scarcely anything here that Raphael would have had to alter to adapt the composition to one of his tapestry cartoons.

Of the dramatic power of this I need add nothing to what has already been said, but as this is the last of his works which we shall examine it may afford an example of some of the characteristics of Giotto's draughtsmanship. For Giotto was one of the greatest masters of line that the world has seen, and the fact that his knowledge of the forms of the figure was comparatively elementary in no way interferes with his greatness. It is not how many facts about an object an artist can record, but how incisive and how harmonious with itself the record is, that constitutes the essence of draughtsmanship.

In considering the qualities of line, three main elements are to be regarded: First, the decorative rhythm, our sense of sight being constructed like our sense of sound, so that certain relations, probably those which are capable of mathematical analysis, are pleasing, and others discordant. Secondly, the significance of line as enabling us imaginatively to reconstruct a real, not necessarily an actual, object from it. The greatest excellence of this quality will be the condensation of the greatest possible suggestion of real form into the simplest, most easily apprehended line; the absence of confusing superfluity on the one hand, and mechanical, and therefore meaningless simplicity, on the other. Finally, we may regard line as a gesture, which impresses us as a direct revelation of the artist's personality in the same way that handwriting does.

Now, with Giotto, beautiful as his line undoubtedly is, it is not the first quality, the decorative rhythm, that most immediately impresses us. That is not the object of such deliberate and conscious research as with some artists. It is in its significance for the expression of form with the utmost lucidity, the most logical interrelation of parts that his line is so impressive. Here, for instance, in the figure of the kneeling women, the form is expressed with perfect clearness; we feel at once the relation of the shoulders to one another, the relation of the torso to the pelvis, the main position of the thighs, and all this is conveyed by a curve of incredible simplicity capable of instant apprehension. To record so much with such economy requires not only a rare imaginative grasp of structure, but a manual dexterity which makes the story of Giotto's O perfectly credible should one care to believe it.

Giotto's line, regarded as an habitual gesture, is chiefly striking for its breadth and dignity. It has the directness, the absence of preciosity, which belong to a generous and manly nature. The large sweeping curves of his loose and full draperies are in part the direct outcome of this attitude.

It is difficult to avoid the temptation to say of Giotto that he was the greatest artist that ever lived, a phrase which has been used of too many masters to retain its full emphasis. But at least he was the most prodigious phenomenon in the known history of art. Starting with little but the crude realism of Cimabue, tempered by the effete accomplishment of the Byzantines,[1] to have created an art capable of expressing the whole range of human emotions; to have found, almost without a guide, how to treat the raw material of life itself in a style so direct, so pliant to the idea, and yet so essentially grandiose and heroic; to have guessed intuitively almost all the principles of representation which it required nearly two centuries of enthusiastic research to establish scientifically— to have accomplished all this is surely a more astounding performance than any other one artist has ever achieved.

But the fascination Giotto's art exercises is due in part to his position in the development of modern culture. Coming at the same time as Dante, he shares with him the privilege of seeing life as a single, self-consistent, and systematic whole. It was a moment of equilibrium between the conflicting tendencies of human activity, a moment when such men as Dante and Giotto could exercise to the full their critical and analytical powers without destroying the unity of a cosmic theory based on theology. Such a moment was in its nature transitory: the free use of all the faculties which the awakening to a new self-consciousness had

[1] This passage now seems to me to underestimate the work of Giotto's predecessors with which we are now much better acquainted (1920).

aroused, was bound to bring about antitheses which became more and more irreconcilable as time went on. Only one other artist in later times was able again to rise, by means of the conception of natural law, to a point whence life could be viewed as a whole. Even so, it was by a more purely intellectual effort, and Leonardo da Vinci could not keep the same genial but shrewd sympathy for common humanity which makes Giotto's work so eternally refreshing.

THE ART OF FLORENCE[1]

THE "artistic temperament"—as used in the press and the police court, these words betray a general misunderstanding of the nature of art, and of the artist whenever he becomes fully conscious of its purpose. The idea of the artist as the plaything of whim and caprice, a hypersensitive and incoherent emotionalist, is, no doubt, true of a certain class of men, many of whom practise the arts; nothing could be further from a true account of those artists whose work has had the deepest influence on the tradition of art; nothing could be less true of the great artists of the Florentine School.

From the rise of modern art in the thirteenth century till now Florence and France have been the decisive factors in the art of Europe. Without them our art might have reflected innumerable pathetic or dramatic moods, it might have illustrated various curious or moving situations, it would not have attained to the conception of generalised truth of form.

To Florence of the fourteenth and fifteenth centuries and to France of the seventeenth and succeeding centuries we owe the creation of generalised or what, for want of a better word, we may call "intellectual" art.

[1] Burlington Fine Arts Club Exhibition of Florentine Paintings, 1919.

In speaking of intellect it is necessary to discriminate between two distinct modes of its operation. The intellect may seek to satisfy curiosity by observation of the distinctions between one object and another by means of analysis; but it may concern itself with the discovery of fundamental relations between these objects, by the construction of a synthetic system which satisfies the mind, both for its truth to facts and its logical coherence. The artist may employ both these modes. His curiosity about the phenomena of nature may lead him to accurate observation and recognition of the variety and distinctness of characters, but he also seeks to construe these distinct forms into such a coherent whole as will satisfy the æsthetic desire for unity. Perhaps the processes employed by the artist may not be identical with the intellectual processes of science, but it is evident that they present a very close analogy to them.

It is a curious fact that at the beginning of the fifteenth century in Italy, art was deeply affected by both kinds of intellectual activity. Curiosity about natural forms in all their variety and complexity—*naturalism* in the modern sense—first manifested itself in European art in Flanders, France, and North Italy about the second decade of the fifteenth century. It appears that Italy actually led the way in this movement, and that Lombardy was the point of origin. Pisanello and Jacopo Bellini are the great exemplars in Italy of this idea of exploring indefatigably and somewhat recklessly all those detailed aspects of nature which their predecessors, occupied in the grand Giottesque style, had scorned to notice.

In Florence, too, this impulse was undoubtedly felt, but it is the great distinction of the Florentine artists that, however much their curiosity about particular forms may have been excited, their high intellectual passion for abstract ideas impelled them more to the study of some general principles underlying all appearance. They refused to admit the given facts of nature except in so far as they could become amenable to the generalising power of their art. Facts had to be digested into form before they were allowed into the system.

We can get an idea of what Florence of the fifteenth century meant for the subsequent tradition of European art if we consider that if it had not been for Florence the art of Italy might have been not altogether unlike the art of Flanders and the Rhine—a little more rhythmical, a little more gracious, perhaps, but fundamentally hardly more significant.

Although this typically Florentine attitude defined itself most clearly under the stress of naturalism it was, of course, already characteristic of earlier Florentine art. Giotto, indeed, had left the tradition of formal completeness so firmly fixed in Florence that whatever new material had to be introduced it could only be introduced into a clearly recognised system of design.

Of Giotto's own work we rarely get a sight in England, the National Gallery having missed the one great chance of getting him represented some twenty years ago. But though Lady Jekyll's single figure of Christ can by its nature give no idea of his amazing and almost unequalled power of discovering unexpected inevitabilities of formal relations, it gives none the less something of Giotto's peculiar beauty of drawing, wherein the completest reality is attained without any attempted verisimilitude. In Mr. Harris's Bernardo Daddi we get nearer perhaps to Giotto as a composer, and even in his Giovanni da Milano, in spite of some Lombard grossness and sentimentality, the great tradition still lives.

Masaccio, represented here by Mr. Rickett's single figure, is one of the most mysterious personalities in art, and typically Florentine. His mystery lies partly in our ignorance about him, partly in the difficulty of grasping the rapidity of action, the precocity, of genius such as his. Coming at the very beginning of the naturalistic movement he seized with a strange complacency and ease upon the new material it offered, but—and this is what astounds one—he instantly discovered how to assimilate it perfectly to the formal requirements of design. So that not only the discovery of the new material, but its digestion was with him a simultaneous and almost instantaneous process. He was helped perhaps by the fact that the new naturalism was as yet only a general perception of new aspects of natural form. It was left for his younger contemporaries to map out the new country methodically—to the group of adventurous spirits—Brunelleschi, Donatello, Castagno, and Ucello—who founded modern science, and gave to the understanding of classic art a methodical basis. It is in this group that the fierce intellectual passion of the Florentine genius manifests itself most clearly. Perspective and anatomy were the two studies which promised to reveal to them the secrets of natural form. The study of anatomy exemplifies mainly the aspect of curiosity, though even in this the desire to find the underlying principles of appearance is evident— on the other hand perspective, to its first discoverers, appeared to promise far more than an aid to verisimilitude, it may have seemed a visual revelation of the structure of space, and through that a key to the construction of pictorial space.

To our more penetrating study of æsthetic (for of all sciences, æsthetic has been the greatest laggard) it is evident that neither perspective nor anatomy has any very immediate bearing upon art—both of them are means of ascertaining facts, and the question of art begins where the question of fact ends. But artists have always had to excite themselves with some kind of subsidiary intoxicant, and perspective and anatomy, while they were still in their infancy, acted admirably as stimulants. That they have by now become, for most artists, the dreariest of sedatives may make it difficult to conceive this. But at all events in that first generation they excited their devotees to an ardent search for abstract unity of design. And this excitement went on to the next generation as exemplified by the works of the Umbro-Florentines—Piero della Francesca and Signorelli—and in Florence itself of Pollajuolo.

But the scientific spirit once aroused was destined not to remain for long so stimulating and helpful an assistant to the creation of design. It was bound in the end to start trains of thought too complex and too absorbing to occupy a subordinate place. Already in the rank and file of Florentine artists, the Ghirlandajos, Filippino Lippis, and their kindred, mere curiosity— naïve literalism—had undermined the tradition, so that towards the last quarter of the century hardly any artist knew how to design intelligibly on the scale of a fresco, whereas the merest duffer of the fourteenth century could be certain of the volumes and quantities of his divisions.

But it is with Leonardo da Vinci that the higher aspects of the scientific spirit first came into conflict with art. Doubtless this conflict is not fundamental nor final, but only an apparent result of human limitations; but to one who, like Leonardo, first had a Pisgah prospect of that immense territory, to the exploration of which four centuries of the intensest human effort have been devoted without yet getting in sight of its boundaries—to such a man it was almost inevitable that the scientific content of art should assume an undue significance. Up till Leonardo one can say that the process of digesting the new-found material into æsthetic form had kept pace with observation, though already in Verrocchio there is a sign of yielding to the crude phenomenon. But with Leonardo himself the organising faculty begins to break down under the stress

of new matter. Leonardo himself shared to the full
the Florentine passion for abstraction, but it was
inevitable that he should be dazzled and fascinated by
the vast prospects that opened before his intellectual
gaze. It was inevitable that where such vast masses of
new particulars revealed themselves to his curiosity
their claim for investigation should be the most insistent.
Not but what Leonardo did recognise the necessity
for his art of some restriction and choice. His keen
observation had revealed to him the whole gamut of
atmospheric colour which first became a material for
design under Monet and his followers. But having
described a picture which would exactly correspond to
a French painting of 1870, he rejects the whole of this
new material as unsuitable for art. But even his rejection
was not really a recognition of the claims of form, but
only, alas! of another scientific trend with which his
mind had become possessed. It was his almost prophetic
vision of the possibilities of psychology which determined more than anything else the lines of his work.
In the end almost everything was subordinated to the
idea of a kind of psychological illustration of dramatic
themes—an illustration which was not to be arrived at
by an instinctive reconstruction from within, but by
deliberate analytic observation. Now in so far as the
movements of the soul could be interpreted by movements of the body as a whole, the new material might
lend itself readily to plastic construction, but the minuter
and even more psychologically significant movements
of facial expression demanded a treatment which
hardly worked for æsthetic unity. It involved a new
use of light and shade, which in itself tended to break
down the fundamental divisions of design, though later
on Caravaggio and Rembrandt managed, not very
successfully, to pull it round so as to become the material
for the basic rhythm. And in any case the analytic
trend of Leonardo's mind became too much accentuated

to allow of a successful synthesis. Michelangelo, to some extent, and Raphael still more, did, of course, do much to re-establish a system of design on an enlarged basis which would admit of some of Leonardo's new content, but one might hazard the speculation that European art has hardly yet recovered from the shock which Leonardo's passion for psychological illustration delivered. Certainly literalism and illustration have through all these centuries been pressing dangers to art—dangers which it has been the harder to resist in that they allow of an appeal to that vast public to whom the language of form is meaningless.

In Florentine art, then, one may see at happy moments of equilibrium the supreme advantages of intellectual art and at other and less fortunate moments the dangers which beset so difficult an endeavour. It was after all a Florentine who made the best prophecy of the results of modern æsthetic when he said: "Finally, good painting is a music and a melody which intellect only can appreciate and that with difficulty."

THE JACQUEMART - ANDRÉ COLLECTION[1]

THE Jacquemart-André collection is not merely one of those accumulations of the art of the past by which it has become the fashion for rich people to impose themselves on the wonder of an ignorant public. It shows that the lady who created it did so partly, at all events, because of a quite personal and intimate love of beautiful things, a love which did not have to seek for its justification and support in the opinion of the world.

The three pictures discussed here are proof of the sincerity and courage of Mdme. André's artistic convictions. They offer scarcely any foothold for the sentimental and associative understanding of pictures.

[1] Burlington Magazine, 1914.

The "St. George" of Paolo Ucello might, it is true, be taken as a "naïve," "quaint," or "primitive" rendering of an "old world" legend—indeed, whilst I was admiring it I gathered from the comments of those who lingered before it for a few seconds that this was the general attitude—but to do so would be to misunderstand the picture completely. Ucello, in fact, lends himself to misunderstanding, and Vasari, with his eye to literary picturesqueness, has done his best to put us off the scent. He made him an "original," a harmless, ingenious, slightly ridiculous crank—gifted, no doubt,—but one whose gifts were wasted by reason of his crankiness. And the legend created by Vasari has stuck. Ucello has always seemed to be a little aside from the main road of art, an agreeable, amusing diversion, one that we can enjoy with a certain humorous and patronising detachment, as we enjoy the innocence of some mediæval chronicler. Ucello, I admit, has lent himself to this misunderstanding because from every other point of view but that of pure design he comes up to the character Vasari has made current. No artist was ever so helpless as he at the dramatic presentment of his theme. Nothing can well be imagined less like a battle than his battle pieces, nor if we think of the Deluge would our wildest fancies have ever conceived anything remotely resembling the scene which he painted with such literal precision, with such a mass of inconclusive and improbable invention, in the Chiostro Verde of Sta. Maria Novella.

The idea of verisimilitude is entirely foreign to him. And here comes in the oddity and irony of his situation. He was the first or almost the first great master of linear perspective. The study of perspective became so engrossing to him that according to Vasari it wasted his talent as an artist.

Now perspective is the scientific statement of the nature of visual appearance. To the modern artist it becomes an occasional assistance in giving to his images an air of verisimilitude. Wherever a strict adherence to the laws of perspective would give to his objects a strange or unlikely look he frankly neglects it. But to Ucello perspective seemed, perhaps wrongly, to have an altogether different value. To him it appears to have been a method of recreating a visual world. That is to say, he took certain data of appearance from observation, and by handling them according to the laws of perspective he created a world, which, owing to the simplicity of his data and the rigid application of his laws, has far less resemblance to what we see than his contemporaries and predecessors had contrived by rule of thumb. Had he taken the whole of the data of observed form the application of the laws of perspective would have become impossible, and he would have been thrown back upon imitative realism and the literal acceptance of appearance. Such was indeed what happened to the painters of Flanders and the north, and such has become the usual method of modern realistic art. But nothing was more abhorrent to the spirit of fifteenth-century Florence than such an acceptance of the merely casual, and nothing is more fundamentally opposed to the empirical realism of a Van Eyck or a Frith than the scientific and abstract realism of Paolo Ucello.

This passion, then, for an abstract and theoretical completeness of rendering led Ucello to simplify the data of observed form to an extraordinary extent, and his simplification anticipates in a curious way that of the modern cubists, as one may see from the treatment of his horses in the National Gallery battle-piece.

It is one of the curiosities of the psychology of the artist that he is generally trying very hard to do something which has nothing to do with what he actually accomplishes; that the fundamental quality of his work seems to come out unconsciously as a by-product of his conscious activity. And so it was in Ucello's case. If one had asked him what his perspective was for, he would probably have said that when once it was completely mastered it would enable the artist to create at will any kind of visual whole, and that this would have the same completeness, the same authenticity as an actual scene. As a matter of fact such a conception is unrealisable; the problem is too complex for solution in this way, and what happened to Ucello was that the simplifications and abstractions imposed upon his observation of nature by the desire to construct his whole scene perspectively, really set free in him his power of creating a purely æsthetic organisation of form. And it is this, in fact, that makes his pictures so remarkable. In the Jacquemart-André picture, for instance, we see how the complex whole which such a scene as the legend of S. George suggests is reduced to terms of astounding simplicity; saint, horse, dragon, princess are all seen in profile because the problems of representation had to be approached from their simplest aspect. The landscape is reduced to a system of rectilinear forms seen at right angles to the picture plane for the same reason.

And out of the play of these almost abstract forms mainly rectangular, with a few elementary curves repeated again and again, Ucello has constructed the most perfect, the most amazingly subtle harmony. In Ucello's hands painting becomes almost as abstract, almost as pure an art as architecture. And as his feeling for the interplay of forms, the rhythmic disposition of planes, was of the rarest and finest, the most removed from anything trivial or merely decorative (in the vulgar sense), he passes by means of this power of formal organisation into a region of feeling entirely remote from that which is suggested if we regard his work as mere illustration. Judged as illustration the "S. George" is quaint, innocent and slightly childish; as design it must rank among the great masterpieces.

Two other pictures in the Jacquemart-André collection illustrate the same spirit of uncompromising æsthetic adventure which distinguishes one branch of the Florentine school of the fifteenth century, and lifts it above almost all that was being attempted elsewhere in Italy even at this period of creative exuberance.

Baldovinetti was at one time in close contact with Ucello, and of all his works the "Madonna and Child" in the Jacquemart-André collection is the most heroically uncompromising. No doubt he accepted more material directly from nature than Ucello did. He was beginning to explore the principles of atmospheric perspective which were destined ultimately to break up the unity of pictorial design, but everything that he takes is used with the same spirit of obedience to the laws of architectonic harmony. The spacing of this design, the relations of volume of the upright mass of the Virgin's figure to the spaces of sky and landscape have the unmistakable interdependence of great design. Only a great creative artist could have discovered so definite a relationship. The great mass of the rocky hill in the landscape and the horizontal lines of the Child's figure play into the central idea with splendid effect. Only in the somewhat rounded and insensitive modelling of the Virgin's face does the weakness of Baldovinetti's genius betray itself. The contours are everywhere magnificently plastic; only when he tries to create the illusion of plastic relief by modelling, Baldovinetti becomes literal and uninspired. In his profile portrait in the National Gallery he relies fortunately almost entirely on the plasticity of the contour—in his late "Trinità" at the Accademia in Florence the increasing desire for imitative realism has already gone far to destroy this quality.

The third picture which I have taken as illustrating my theme is not, it is true, Florentine, but its author, Signorelli, kept so constantly in touch with the scientific realists of Florence that he may be counted almost as one of them, nor indeed did any of them surpass him in uncompromising fidelity to the necessities of pure design. Certainly there is nothing of the flattering or seductive qualities of the common run of Umbrian art in this robust and audacious composition, in which everything is arranged as it were concentrically around the imposing mass of the Virgin's figure. The gestures interpreted psychologically are not on the same imaginative plane as the design itself. Signorelli was ill at ease in interpreting any states but those of great tension, and here the gestures are meant to be playful and intimate. As in the Ucello, the illustrative pretext is at variance with the design which it serves; and as in the Ucello, the design itself, the scaffolding of the architectonic structure, is really what counts.

DÜRER AND HIS CONTEMPORARIES [1]

IT is a habit of the human mind to make to itself symbols in order to abbreviate its admiration for a class. So Dürer has come to stand for German art somewhat as Raphael once stood for Italian. Such symbols attract to themselves much of the adoration which more careful worshippers would distribute throughout the Pantheon, and it becomes difficult to appreciate them justly without incurring the charge of iconoclasm. But this, in Dürer's case, is the more difficult because, whatever one's final estimate of his art, his personality is at once so imposing and so attractive, and has been so endeared to us by familiarity, that something of this personal attachment has transferred itself to our æsthetic judgment.

The letters from Venice and the Diary of his journey

[1] Introduction to Dürer's Letters and Diary. Merrymount Press, Boston (1909).

in the Netherlands, which form the matter of this volume, are indeed the singularly fortunate means for this pleasant discourse with the man himself. They reveal Dürer as one of the distinctively modern men of the Renaissance: intensely, but not arrogantly, conscious of his own personality; accepting with a pleasant ease the universal admiration of his genius—a personal admiration, too, of an altogether modern kind; careful of his fame as one who foresaw its immortality. They show him as having, though in a far less degree, something of Leonardo da Vinci's scientific interest, certainly as having a quick, though naïve curiosity about the world and a quite modern freedom from superstition. It is clear that his dominating, and yet kindly personality, no less than his physical beauty and distinction, made him the centre of interest wherever he went. His easy and humorous good-fellowship, of which the letters to Pirkheimer are eloquent, won for him the admiring friendship of the best men of his time. To all these characteristics we must add a deep and sincere religious feeling, which led him to side with the leaders of the Reformation, a feeling that comes out in his passionate sense of loss when he thinks that Luther is about to be put to death, and that prompted him to write a stirring letter to Erasmus, in which he urged him to continue the work of reform. For all that, there is no trace in him of either Protestantism or Puritanism. He was perhaps fortunate—certainly as an artist he was fortunate—in living at a time when the line of cleavage between the Reformers and the Church was not yet so marked as to compel a decisive choice. The symbolism of the Church still had for him its old significance, as yet quickened and not discredited by the reformer's energy. But intense as Dürer's devotion was, his religious feeling found its way to effective artistic expression only upon one side, namely, the brooding sense which accompanied it, of the imminence

F

and terror of death. How much more definite is the
inspiration in the drawing of " Death on a Horse "—·
in the British Museum,—in the " Knight, Death and
the Devil," and in the allied " Melancholia," than it
is in his renderings of the Virgin or indeed of any of
the scenes of Christian legend! It is this feeling, too,
which gives to his description of his mother's death
its almost terrible literary beauty and power. Nor in
the estimate of Dürer's character must one leave out
the touching affection and piety which the family history
written by him in 1524 reveals.

So much that is attractive and endearing in the man
cannot but react upon our attitude to his work—has
done so, perhaps, ever since his own day; and it is
difficult to get far enough away from Dürer the man
to be perfectly just to Dürer the artist. But if we make
the attempt, it becomes clear, I think, that Dürer cannot take rank in the highest class of creative geniuses.
His position is none the less of great importance and
interest for his relation on the one hand to the Gothic
tradition of his country, and on the other to the newly
perceived splendours of the Italian Renaissance.

Much must depend on our estimate of his last work,
the " Four Apostles," at Munich. In that he summed
up all that the patient and enthusiastic labour of a
lifetime had taught him. If we regard that as a work
of the highest beauty, if we can conscientiously put
it beside the figures of the Sistine Chapel, beside the
Saints of Mantegna, or Signorelli, or Piero della Francesca, then indeed Dürer's labour was crowned with
success; but if we find in it rather a careful exposition
of certain theoretical principles, if we find that the
matter is not entirely transfused with the style, if we
find a conflict between a certain naïve crudity of vision
and a straining after the grand manner, then we have
to say that Dürer's art was the outcome of a magnificent
and heroic but miscalculated endeavour.

It is one of the ironies of history that the Romans, the only Philistine people among Mediterranean races, should have been the great means of transmitting to the modern world that culture which they themselves despised, and that the Germans should have laboured so long and hard to atone for the heroism of their ancestors in resisting that beneficent loss of liberty. Nuremberg of the fifteenth century was certainly given over to the practice of fine art with a pathetic enthusiasm, and it remains as a sad but instructive proof of how little good-will and industry avail by themselves in such matters. The worship of mere professional skill and undirected craftsmanship is there seen pushed to its last conclusions, and the tourist's wonder is prompted by the sight of stone carved into the shapes of twisted metal, and wood simulating the intricacies of confectionery, his admiration is canvassed by every possible perversion of technical dexterity. Not " What a thing is done ! " but, " How difficult it must have been to do it ! " is the exclamation demanded.

Of all that perverted technical ingenuity which flaunts itself in the wavering stonework of a Kraft or the crackling woodwork of a Storr, Dürer was inevitably the heir. He grew up in an atmosphere where the acrobatic feats of technique were looked on with admiration rather than contempt. Something of this clung to him through life, and he is always recognised as the prince of craftsmen, the consummate technician. In all this side of Dürer's art we recognise the last over-blown efflorescence of the mediæval craftsmanship of Germany, of the apprentice system and the " master " piece; but that Gothic tradition had still left in it much that was sound and sincere. Drawing still retained something of the blunt, almost brutal frankness of statement, together with the sense of the characteristic which marked its earlier period. And it is perhaps this inheritance of Gothic directness of statement, this

Gothic realism, that accounts for what is ultimately of most value in Dürer's work. There exists in the Kunsthistorisches Akademie at Vienna a painting of a man, dated 1394, which shows how much of Dürer's portraiture was already implicit in the Nuremburg school. In this remarkable work, executed, if we may trust the date, nearly a century before Dürer, there is almost everything that interests us in Dürer's portraits. Indeed, it has to an even greater extent that half-humorous statement of the characteristic, that outrageous realism that makes the vivid appeal of the Oswold Krell, and the absence of which in Dürer's last years makes the Holtschuer such a tiresome piece of brilliant delineation.

Dürer was perhaps the greatest infant prodigy among painters, and the drawing of himself at the age of twelve shows how early he had mastered that simple and abrupt sincerity of Gothic draughtsmanship. One is inclined to say that in none of his subsequent work did he ever surpass this in all that really matters, in all that concerns the essential vision and its adequate presentment. He increased his skill until it became the wonder of the world and entangled him in its seductions; his intellectual apprehension was indefinitely heightened, and his knowledge of natural appearances became encyclopædic.

What, then, lies at the root of Dürer's art is this Gothic sense of the characteristic, already menaced by the professional bravura of the late Gothic craftsman. The superstructure is what Dürer's industry and intellectual acquisitiveness, acting in the peculiar conditions of his day, brought forth. It is in short what distinguishes him as the pioneer of the Renaissance in Germany. This new endeavour was in two directions, one due mainly to the trend of native ideas, the other to Italian influence. The former was concerned mainly with a new kind of realism. In place of the older Gothic

realism with its naïve and self-confident statement of
the salient characteristic of things seen, this new realism
strove at complete representation of appearance by means
of perspective, at a more searching and complete investigation of form, and a fuller relief in light and shade.

To some extent these aims were followed also by
the Italians, and with even greater scientific ardour:
all the artists of Europe were indeed striving to master
the complete power of representation. But in Italy
this aim was never followed exclusively; it was constantly modified and controlled by the idea of design,
that is to say, of expression by means of the pure
disposition of contours and masses, and by the perfection and ordering of linear rhythm. This notion of
design as something other than representation was
indeed the common inheritance of European art from
the mediæval world, but in Italy the principles of
design were more profoundly embedded in tradition,
its demands were more clearly felt, and each succeeding
generation was quite as deeply concerned with the
perfection of design as with the mastery of representation. In the full Renaissance, indeed, this idea of
design became the object of conscious and deliberate
study, and the decadence of Italian art came about,
not through indifference to the claims of artistic expression, but through a too purely intellectual and conscious
study of them. The northern and especially the Teutonic
artists, who had not inherited so strongly this architectonic sense, made indeed heroic efforts to acquire it,
sometimes by the futile method of direct imitation of
a particular style, sometimes—and this is the case with
Dürer—by a serious effort of æsthetic intelligence.
But on the whole the attempt must be judged to have
failed, and northern art has drifted gradually towards
the merely photographic vision.

Dürer strove strenuously in both these directions.
He unquestionably added immensely to the knowledge

of actual form and to the power of representation, but his eagerness led him to regard quantity of form rather than its quality. With him drawing became a means of making manifest the greatest possible amount of form, the utmost roundness of relief, and his studies in pure design failed to keep pace with this. In the end he could not use to significant purpose the increased material at his disposal, and from the point of view of pure design his work actually falls short of that of his predecessor, Martin Schongauer, who indeed was benefited by lacking Dürer's power of representation.

From this point of view it may be worth while to examine in some detail Dürer's relations to Italian art. The earliest definite example of his study of Italian art is in 1494, when he was probably in Venice for the first time. It is a copy in pen and ink of an engraving of the " Death of Orpheus " by some follower of Mantegna. The engraving is not the work of a great artist, and Dürer's copy shows his superior skill in the rendering of form; but even here he has failed to realise the beauty of spatial arrangement in the original, and his desire to enrich the design with many skilfully drawn and convincing details results in a distinct weakening of the dramatic effect. Again, in the same year we have two drawings from engravings, this time by Mantegna himself. It is easy to understand that of all Italians, Mantegna should have been the most sympathetic to Dürer, and that he should have regretted more than any other ill-fortune of his life,—more even than the similar fate that prevented his meeting Schongauer,—Mantegna's death just when he was setting out to Mantua to learn from the great master. What Dürer saw in Mantegna was his clear decision of line and his richly patterned effect. In his pen-and-ink copies he tries to surpass the original in both these ways, and indeed the effect is of greater complexity, with more fullness and roundness of form. Where

Mantegna is content with a firm statement of the generalised contour of a limb, Dürer will give a curve for each muscle. There is in Dürer's copies a mass of brilliant detail; each part is in a sense more convincingly real; but in doing this something of the unity of rhythm and the easy relations of planes has been lost, and on the whole the balance is against the copyist. It is curious that when in time Rembrandt came to copy Mantegna he took the other way, and actually heightened the dramatic effect by minute readjustments of planning, and by a wilful simplification of the line.

Dürer evidently felt a profound reverence for Mantegna's designs, for he has altered them but little, and one might well imagine that even Dürer could scarcely improve upon such originals. But it is even more instructive to study his work upon the so-called Tarocchi engravings. Here the originals were not executed by an artist of first-rate ability, though the designs have much of Cossa's splendid style. Dürer seems, therefore, to have felt no particular constraint about altering them. His alterations show us clearly what it was that he saw in the originals and what he missed. In all these figures Dürer gives increased verisimilitude: his feet are like actual feet, not the schematic abstract of a foot that contents the Italian engraver; his poses are more casual, less formal and symmetrical; and his draperies are more ingeniously disposed; but none the less, from the point of view of the expression of imaginative truth, there is not one of Dürer's figures which equals the original, not one in which some essential part of the idea is not missed or at least less clearly stated. In general the continuity of the contour is lost sight of and the rhythm frittered away. In the Pope, for instance, Dürer loses all the grave sedateness of the original by breaking the symmetry of the pose, its squareness and immovable aplomb. And with this goes, in spite of the increased verisimilitude, the sense of reality. In the " Knight and Page " not only is the movement of the knight missed by correcting a distortion in the original, but the balance of the composition is lost by displacing the page. In the "Primum Mobile" the ecstatic rush of the figure is lost by slight corrections in the pose and by giving to the floating drapery too complicated a design. It would be tedious to go through these copies in detail, but enough has been said to show how hard it was for Dürer, absorbed by his new curiosity in representation, to grasp those primary and elemental principles of design which were inherent in the Italian tradition.

About the same time we find Dürer studying both Pollajuolo and Lorenzo di Credi. The copy of Pollajuolo is not a good example of Dürer's art; it certainly misses the tension and inner life of Pollajuolo's nudes. The Lorenzo di Credi, as might be expected, is in many ways more than adequate to the original, though as compared even with Credi, Dürer has not a clear sense of the correlation of linear elements in the design.

The next stage in Dürer's connection with Italian art is his intimacy with Jacopo de' Barbari, who was settled in Nuremberg. From 1500 to 1505 this influence manifests itself clearly in Dürer's work. Unfortunately Barbari was too second-rate an artist to help him much in the principles of design, though he doubtless stimulated him to pursue those scientific investigations into the theory of human proportions which held out the delusive hope of reducing art to a branch of mathematics.

It was not, however, until his second visit to Venice that Dürer realised the inferiority, at all events, of Barbari, and it was then that, through his amiable relations with Giovanni Bellini, he came nearer than at any other moment of his life to penetrating the mysteries of Italian design. It is in the letters from

Venice, written at this time, that his connection with the Venetian artists is made clear, and a study of those writings will be found to illuminate in a most interesting way Dürer's artistic consciousness, and help to answer the question of how he regarded his own work when seen in comparison with the Venetians, and in what manner the Venetians regarded this wonder worker from the north.

EL GRECO[1]

MR. HOLMES has risked a good deal in acquiring for the nation the new El Greco. The foresight and understanding necessary to bring off such a *coup* are not the qualities that we look for from a Director of the National Gallery. Patriotic people may even be inclined to think that the whole proceeding smacks too much of the manner in which Dr. Bode in past ages built up the Kaiser Friedrich Museum, largely at the expense of English collections. Even before the acquisition of the El Greco there were signs that Mr. Holmes did not fully understand the importance of " muddling through." And now with the El Greco he has given the British public an electric shock. People gather in crowds in front of it, they argue and discuss and lose their tempers. This might be intelligible enough if the price were known to be fabulous, but, so far as I am aware, the price has not been made known, so that it is really about the picture that people get excited. And what is more, they talk about it as they might talk about some contemporary picture, a thing with which they have a right to feel delighted or infuriated as the case may be—it is not like most old pictures, a thing classified and museumified, set altogether apart from life, an object for vague and listless reverence, but an actual living thing, expressing something with

[1] Athenæum, 1920.

which one has got either to agree or disagree. Even
if it should not be the superb masterpiece which most
of us think it is, almost any sum would have been
well spent on a picture capable of provoking such
fierce æsthetic interest in the crowd.

That artists are excited—never more so—is no
wonder, for here is an old master who is not merely
modern, but actually appears a good many steps ahead
of us, turning back to show us the way. Immortality
if you like! But the public—what is it that makes
them " sit up " so surprisingly, one wonders. What
makes this El Greco " count " with them as surely
no Old Master ever did within memory? First, I
suspect, the extraordinary completeness of its realisation. Even the most casual spectator, passing among
pictures which retire discreetly behind their canvases,
must be struck by the violent attack of these forms,
by a relief so out-standing that by comparison the
actual scene, the gallery and one's neighbours are
reduced to the key of a Whistlerian Nocturne. Partly,
for we must face the fact, the melodramatic apparatus;
the " horrid " rocks, the veiled moon, the ecstatic
gestures. Not even the cinema star can push expression
further than this. Partly, no doubt, the clarity and the
balanced rhythm of the design, the assurance and grace
of the handling; for, however little people may be
conscious of it, formal qualities do affect their reaction
to a picture, though they may pass from them almost
immediately to its other implications. And certainly
here, if anywhere formal considerations must obtrude
themselves even on the most unobservant. The extraordinary emphasis and amplitude of the rhythm, which
thus gathers up into a few sweeping diagonals the whole
complex of the vision, is directly exciting and stimulating. It affects one like an irresistible melody, and
makes that organisation of all the parts into a single
whole, which is generally so difficult for the uninitiated,

an easy matter for once. El Greco, indeed, puts the problem of form and content in a curious way. The artist, whose concern is ultimately and, I believe, exclusively with form, will no doubt be so carried away by the intensity and completeness of the design, that he will never even notice the melodramatic and sentimental content which shocks or delights the ordinary man. It is none the less an interesting question, though it is rather one of artists' psychology than of æsthetics, to inquire in what way these two things, the melodramatic expression of a high-pitched religiosity and a peculiarly intense feeling for plastic unity and rhythmic amplitude, were combined in El Greco's work; even to ask whether there can have been any casual connection between them in the workings of El Greco's spirit.

Strange and extravagantly individual as El Greco seems, he was not really an isolated figure, a miraculous and monstrous apparition thrust into the even current of artistic movement. He really takes his place alongside of Bernini as a great exponent of the Baroque idea in figurative art. And the Baroque idea goes back to Michelangelo. Formally, its essence both in art and architecture was the utmost possible enlargement of the unit of design. One can see this most easily in architecture. To Bramante the façade of a palace was made up of a series of storeys, each with its pilasters and windows related proportionally to one another, but each a co-ordinate unit of design. To the Baroque architect a façade was a single storey with pilasters going the whole height, and only divided, as it were, by an afterthought into subordinate groups corresponding to the separate storeys. When it came to sculpture and painting the same tendency expressed itself by the discovery of such movements as would make the parts of the body, the head, trunk, limbs, merely so many subordinate divisions of a single unit.

Now to do this implied extremely emphatic and marked poses, though not necessarily violent in the sense of displaying great muscular strain. Such poses correspond as expression to marked and excessive mental states, to conditions of ecstasy, or agony or intense contemp'ation. But even more than to any actual poses resulting from such states, they correspond to a certain accepted and partly conventional language of gesture. They are what we may call rhetorical poses, in that they are not so much the result of the emotions as of the desire to express these emotions to the on-looker.

When the figure is draped the Baroque idea becomes particularly evident. The artists seek voluminous and massive garments which under the stress of an emphatic pose take heavy folds passing in a single diagonal sweep from top to bottom of the whole figure. In the figure of Christ in the National Gallery picture El Greco has established such a diagonal, and has so arranged the light and shade that he gets a state-ment of the same general direction twice over, in the sleeve and in the drapery of the thigh.

Bernini was a consummate master of this method of amplifying the unit, but having once set up the great wave of rhythm which held the figure in a single sweep, he gratified his florid taste by allowing elaborate embroidery in the subordinate divisions, feeling per-fectly secure that no amount of exuberance would destroy the firmly established scaffolding of his design.

Though the psychology of both these great rhetori-cians is infinitely remote from us, we tolerate more easily the gloomy and terrible extravagance of El Greco's melodrama than the radiant effusiveness and amiability of Bernini's operas.

But there is another cause which accounts for our profound difference of feeling towards these two artists. Bernini undoubtedly had a great sense of design, but he was also a prodigious artistic acrobat, capable of feats of dizzying audacity, and unfortunately he loved popularity and the success which came to him so inevitably. He was not fine enough in grain to distinguish between his great imaginative gifts and the superficial virtuosity which made the crowd, including his Popes, gape with astonishment. Consequently he expressed great inventions in a horribly impure technical language. El Greco, on the other hand, had the good fortune to be almost entirely out of touch with the public—one picture painted for the king was sufficient to put him out of court for the rest of his life. And in any case he was a singularly pure artist, he expressed his idea with perfect sincerity, with complete indifference to what effect the right expression might have on the public. At no point is there the slightest compromise with the world; the only issue for him is between him and his idea. Nowhere is a violent form softened, nowhere is the expressive quality of brushwork blurred in order to give versimilitude of texture; no harshness of accent is shirked, no crudity of colour opposition avoided, wherever El Greco felt such things to be necessary to the realisation of his idea. It is this magnificent courage and purity, this total indifference to the expectations of the public, that bring him so near to us to-day, when more than ever the artist regards himself as working for ends unguessed at by the mass of his contemporaries. It is this also which accounts for the fact that while nearly every one shudders involuntarily at Bernini's sentimental sugariness, very few artists of to-day have ever realised for a moment how unsympathetic to them is the literary content of an El Greco. They simply fail to notice what his pictures are about in the illustrative sense.

But to return to the nature of Baroque art. The old question here turns up. Did the dog wag his tail because he was pleased, or was he pleased because his tail wagged ? Did the Baroque artists choose ecstatic subjects because they were excited about a certain kind of rhythm, or did they elaborate the rhythm to express a feeling for extreme emotional states ? There is yet another fact which complicates the matter. Baroque art corresponds well enough in time with the Catholic reaction and the rise of Jesuitism, with a religious movement which tended to dwell particularly on these extreme emotional states, and, in fact, the Baroque artists worked in entire harmony with the religious leaders.

This would look as though religion had inspired the artists with a passion for certain themes, and the need to express these had created Baroque art.

I doubt if it was as simple as that. Some action and reaction between the religious ideas of the time and the artists' conception there may have been, but I think the artists would have elaborated the Baroque idea without this external pressure. For one thing, the idea goes back behind Michelangelo to Signorelli, and in his case, at least, one can see no trace of any preoccupation with those psychological states, but rather a pure passion for a particular kind of rhythmic design. Moreover, the general principle of the continued enlargement of the unit of design was bound to occur the moment artists recovered from the debauch of naturalism of the fifteenth century and became conscious again of the demands of abstract design.

In trying thus to place El Greco's art in perspective, I do not in the least disparage his astonishing individual force. That El Greco had to an extreme degree the quality we call genius is obvious, but he was neither so miraculous nor so isolated as we are often tempted to suppose.

The exuberance and abandonment of Baroque art were natural expressions both of the Italian and Spanish natures, but they were foreign to the intellectual severity of the French genius, and it was from France, and in the person of Poussin, that the counterblast came. He, indeed, could tolerate no such rapid simplification of design. He imposed on himself endless scruples and compunctions, making artistic unity the reward of a long process of selection and discovery. His art became difficult and esoteric. People wonder sometimes at the diversity of modern art, but it is impossible to conceive a sharper opposition than that between Poussin and the Baroque. It is curious, therefore, that modern artists should be able to look back with almost equal reverence to Poussin and to El Greco. In part, this is due to Cézanne's influence, for, from one point of view, his art may be regarded as a synthesis of these two apparently adverse conceptions of design. For Cézanne consciously studied both, taking from Poussin his discretion and the subtlety of his rhythm, and from El Greco his great discovery of the permeation of every part of the design with a uniform and continuous plastic theme. The likeness is indeed sometimes startling. One of the greatest critics of our time, von Tschudi —of Swiss origin, I hasten to add, and an enemy of the Kaiser—was showing me El Greco's " Laocoon," which he had just bought for Munich, when he whispered to me, as being too dangerous a doctrine to be spoken aloud even in his private room, " Do you know why we admire El Greco's handling so much? Because it reminds us of Cézanne."

No wonder, then, that for the artist of to-day the new El Greco is of capital importance. For it shows us the master at the height of his powers, at last perfectly aware of his personal conception and daring to give it the completest, most uncompromising expression. That the picture is in a marvellous state of preservation and has been admirably cleaned adds greatly to its value. Dirty yellow varnish no longer interposes here its hallowing influence between the spectator and the artist's original creation. Since the eye can follow every stroke of the brush, the mind can recover the artist's gesture and almost the movements of his mind. For never was work more perfectly transparent to the idea, never was an artist's intention more deliberately and precisely recorded.

THREE PICTURES IN TEMPERA
BY WILLIAM BLAKE[1]

BLAKE'S finished pictures have never received the same attention nor aroused the same admiration as his washdrawings, his wood-cuts, or his engravings. It is difficult to account for this comparative neglect, since they not only show command of a technique which admits of the completest realisation of the idea, but they seem actually to express what was personal to Blake in a purer form than many of his other works, with less admixture of those unfortunate caprices which the false romantic taste of his day imposed too often even on so original and independent a genius. The explanation may perhaps lie in the fact that to most people Blake, for all his inimitable gifts, appears as a divinely inspired amateur rather than as a finished master of his art, and they are willing to tolerate what they regard as his imperfect control of form in media which admit only of hints and suggestions of the artist's vision.

There assuredly never was a more singular, more inexplicable phenomenon than the intrusion, as though by direct intervention of Providence, of this Assyrian spirit into the vapidly polite circles of eighteenth-century London. The fact that, as far as the middle classes of England were concerned, Puritanism had for a century and a half blocked every inlet and outlet of poetical

[1] Burlington Magazine, 1904.

feeling and imaginative conviction save one, may give us a clue to the causes of such a phenomenon. It was the devotion of Puritan England to the Bible, to the Old Testament especially, that fed such a spirit as Blake's directly from the sources of the most primeval, the vastest and most abstract imagery which we possess. Brooding on the vague and tremendous images of Hebrew and Chaldæan poetry, he arrived at such indifference to the actual material world, at such an intimate perception of the elemental forces which sway the spirit with immortal hopes and infinite terrors when it is most withdrawn from its bodily conditions, that what was given to his internal vision became incomparably more definite, more precisely and more clearly articulated, than anything presented to his senses. His forms are the visible counterparts to those words, like *the deep*, *many waters*, *firmament*, *the foundations of the earth*, *pit* and *host*, whose resonant overtones blur and enrich the sense of the Old Testament. Blake's art moves us, if at all, by a similar evocation of vast elemental forces. He deals directly with these spiritual sensations, bringing in from external nature the least possible content which will enable him to create visible forms at all. But though he pushed them to their furthest limits, even he could not transcend the bounds which beset pictorial language; even he was forced to take something of external nature with him into his visionary world, and his wildest inventions are but recombinations and distorted memories of the actual objects of sense.

By the strangest irony, too, the forms which came to his hand as the readiest means of expressing his stupendous conceptions were in themselves the least expressive, the least grandiose, that ever art has dealt with. It was with the worn-out rags of an effete classical tradition long ago emptied of all meaning, and given over to turgid rhetorical display, that Blake had to piece together the visible garments of his majestic and profound ideas. The complete obsession of his nature by these ideas in itself compelled him to this: he was entirely without curiosity about such trivial and ephemeral things as the earth contained. His was the most anti-Hellenic temperament; he had no concern, either gay or serious, with phenomena; they were too transparent to arrest his eye, and that patient and scientific quarrying from the infinite possibilities of nature of just the appropriate forms to convey his ideas was beyond the powers with which nature and the poor traditions of his day supplied him. Tintoretto, who had in some respects a similar temperament, who felt a similar need of conveying directly the revelations of his internal vision, was more happily situated. He was, by comparison, a trivial and vulgar seer, but the richness and expressive power of the forms which lay to his hand in Titian's and Michelangelo's art enabled him to attain a more unquestionable achievement.

But, allowing for circumstances, what Blake did was surely more considerable and implied a greater sheer lift of imaginative effort. That it was an attempt which remained almost without consequences, isolated and incomplete—marred, too, by a certain incoherence and want of reasonable co-ordination—must be allowed, and may perhaps explain why Blake is not universally admitted among our greatest.

The Byzantine style, he declares, was directly and divinely revealed to him; and whether this were so, or whether he obtained it by the dim indications of Ottley's prints, or through illuminated manuscripts, the marvellous fact remains that he did succeed in recovering for a moment that pristine directness and grandeur of expression which puts him beside the great Byzantine designers as the only fit interpreter of Hebrew mythology. His "Flight into Egypt"[1] will at once

[1] Now in the possession of W. Graham Robertson, Esq.

...ES IN TEMPERA

...he subject in the Arena
...ess is, in a sense, decep-
...y from Byzantinism
...rds it, and the two
...re is here but
...still of

recall G
chapel at
tive, for Giotto was working awa
as fast as Blake was working towa
pass one another on the road. For the
little of Giotto's tender human feeling, less
his robust rationalism; what they have in common,
what Blake rediscovered and Giotto inherited, is the
sentiment of supernatural dignity, the hieratic solemnity
and superhuman purposefulness of the gestures. Even
more than in Giotto's version, the Virgin here sits
on the ass as though enthroned in monumental state,
her limbs fixed in the rigid symmetry which oriental
art has used to express complete withdrawal from the
world of sense. No less perfect in its expressiveness
of the strange and exalted mood is the movement,
repeated with such impressive monotony, in the figures
of Joseph and the archangel. It is absurd, we think,
to deny to the man who discovered the lines of these
figures the power of draughtsmanship. Since Giotto's
day scarcely any one has drawn thus—simplification
has been possible only as the last effort of consummate
science refining away the superfluous; but here the
simplification of the forms is the result of an instinctive passionate reaching out for the direct symbol of
the idea.

Blake's art indeed is a test case for our theories
of æsthetics. It boldly makes the plea for art that
it is a language for conveying impassioned thought
and feeling, which takes up the objects of sense as a
means to this end, owing them no allegiance and
accepting from them only the service that they can
render for this purpose. "Poetry," says Blake, "consists in bold, daring, and masterly conceptions; and
shall painting be confined to the sordid drudgery of
facsimile representations of merely mortal and perishing
substances, and not be, as poetry and music are,

180

elevated into its own pro...
visionary conception?"...
solely by the associ...
it imitates is easily...
and architecture...
spirit is...

sphere of invention and
... The theory that art appeals
... ted ideas of the natural objects
... refuted when we consider music
... in those at least the appeal to the
... made directly in a language which has no
other use than that of conveying its own proper ideas
and feelings. But in pictorial art the fallacy that nature
is the mistress instead of the servant, seems almost
ineradicable, and it is difficult to convince people that
increased scientific investigation of phenomena, increased
knowledge of how things present themselves to our
sight, changes the mode but does not necessarily increase
the power, of pictorial expression. The Byzantine
artists, with a knowledge of appearances infinitely less
than that of the average art student of to-day, could
compass the expression of imaginative truths which
our most accomplished realists dare not attempt. The
essential power of pictorial as of all other arts lies
in its use of a fundamental and universal symbolism,
and whoever has the instinct for this can convey his
ideas, though possessed of only the most rudimentary
knowledge of the actual forms of nature; while he
who has it not can by no accumulation of observed
facts add anything to the spiritual treasure of mankind. Of this language of symbolic form in which
the spirit communicates its most secret and indefinable
impulses Blake was an eloquent and persuasive master.
He could use it, too, to the most diverse ends; and
though the sublimity which is based upon dread came
most readily to his mind, he could express, as we have
seen in the " Flight into Egypt," the sublimity of
divine introspection. In the " David and Bathsheba "
he touches a different note, and he shows his true
power of symbolic expression in this, that it is not
by the treatment of the figure itself, not by any ordinary
sensual enticements, that he gives the atmosphere of

voluptuous abandonment. It is rather in the extravagant tropical flowers, in the architecture which itself blossoms with oriental exuberance, in the fiery orange of the clouds seen behind trees preternaturally virid, that the spirit is bewildered with anticipations of extravagant bliss. The picture might be described in Blake's own terminology as the mental abstract of voluptuousness.

All art gives us an experience freed from the disturbing conditions of actual life. Blake's art, more concentrated than most, gives us an experience which is removed more entirely from bodily and physiological accompaniments, and our experience has the purity, the intensity, and the abstraction of a dream.

CLAUDE[1]

IN spite of all the attacks of critics, in spite of the development of emphasis and high flavour in modern romantic landscape, which might well have spoilt us for his cool simplicity, Claude still lives, not, indeed, as one of the gods of the sale-room, but in the hearts of contemplative and undemonstrative people. This is surely an interesting and encouraging fact. It means that a very purely artistic and poetical appeal still finds its response in the absence of all subsidiary interests and attractions. The appeal is, indeed, a very limited one, touching only certain highly self-conscious and sophisticated moods, but it is, within its limits, so sincere and so poignant that Claude's very failings become, as it were, an essential part of its expression. These failings are, indeed, so many and so obvious that it is not to be wondered at if, now and again, they blind even a sensitive nature like Ruskin's to the fundamental beauty and grandeur of Claude's

[1] Burlington Magazine, 1907.

revelation. But we must be careful not to count as failings qualities which are essential to the particular kind of beauty that Claude envisages, though, to be quite frank, it is sometimes hard to make up one's mind whether a particular characteristic is a lucky defect or a calculated negation. Take, for instance, the peculiar *gaucherie* of his articulations. Claude knows less, perhaps, than any considerable landscape painter—less than the most mediocre of modern landscapists—how to lead from one object to another. His foregrounds are covered with clumsily arranged leaves which have no organic growth, and which, as often as not, lie on the ground instead of springing from it. His trees frequently isolate themselves helplessly from their parent soil. In particular, when he wants a *repoussoir* in the foreground at either end of his composition he has recourse to a clumsily constructed old bare trunk, which has little more meaning than a stage property. Even in his composition there are *naïvetés* which may or may not be intentional: sometimes they have the happiest effect, at others they seem not childlike but childish. Such, for instance, is his frequent habit of dividing spaces equally, both vertically and horizontally, either placing his horizontal line half-way up the picture, or a principal building on the central vertical line. At times this seems the last word of a highly subtilised simplicity, of an artifice which conceals itself; at others one cannot be sure that it is not due to incapacity. There is, in fact, a real excuse for Ruskin's exaggerated paradox that Claude's drawings look like the work of a child of ten. There is a whole world of beauty which one must not look for at all in Claude. All that beauty of the sudden and unexpected revelation of an unsuspected truth which the Gothic and Early Renaissance art provides is absent from Claude. As the eye follows his line it is nowhere arrested by a sense of surprise

at its representative power, nor by that peculiar thrill
which comes from the communication of some vital
creative force in the artist. Compare, for instance,
Claude's drawing of mountains, which he knew and
studied constantly, with Rembrandt's. Rembrandt had
probably never seen mountains, but he obtained a
more intimate understanding by the light of his inner
vision than Claude could ever attain to by familiarity
and study. We need not go to Claude's figures, where
he is notoriously feeble and superficially Raphaelesque,
in order to find how weak was his hold upon character,
whatever the object he set himself to interpret. In the
British Museum there is a most careful and elaborate
study of the rocky shores of a stream. Claude has
even attempted here to render the contorted stratifi-
cation of the river-bed, but without any of that intimate
imaginative grasp of the tension and stress which under-
lie the appearance and which Turner could give in a
few hurried scratches. No one, we may surmise, ever
loved trees more deeply than Claude, and we know
that he prided himself on his careful observation of
the difference of their specific characters; and yet he
will articulate their branches in the most haphazard,
perfunctory manner. There is nothing in all Claude's
innumerable drawings which reveals the inner life of
the tree itself, its aspirations towards air and light,
its struggle with gravitation and wind, as one little
drawing by Leonardo da Vinci does.

All these defects might pass more easily in a turbulent
romanticist, hurrying pell mell to get expressed some
moving and dramatic scene, careless of details, so long
as the main movement were ascertained, but there is
none of this fire in Claude. It is with slow ponderation
and deliberate care that he places before us his perfunctory and generalised statements, finishing and
polishing them with relentless assiduity, and not
infrequently giving us details that we do not desire

and which add nothing but platitude to the too prolix statement.

All this and much more the admirer of Claude will be wise to concede to the adversary, and if the latter ask wherein the beauty of a Claude lies he may with more justice than in any other case fall back on the reply of one of Du Maurier's æsthetes, " in the picture." For there is assuredly a kind of beauty which is not only compatible with these defects but perhaps in some degree depends on them. We know and recognise it well enough in literature. To take a random instance. Racine makes Titus say in " Bérénice ": " De mon aimable erreur je suis désabusé." This may be a dull, weak, and colourless mode of expression, but if he had said with Shakespeare, " Now old desire doth in his death-bed lie, and young affection gapes to be his heir," we should feel that it would destroy the particular kind of even and unaccented harmony at which Racine aimed. Robert Bridges, in his essay on Keats, very aptly describes for literature the kind of beauty which we find in Shakespeare: " the power of concentrating all the far-reaching resources of language on one point, so that a single and apparently effortless expression rejoices the æsthetic imagination at the moment when it is most expectant and exacting." That, *ceteris paribus*, applies admirably to certain kinds of design. It corresponds to the nervous touch of a Pollajuolo or a Rembrandt. But Claude's line is almost nerveless and dull. Even when it is most rapid and free it never surprises us by any intimate revelation of character, any summary indications of the central truth. But it has a certain inexpressive beauty of its own. It is never elegant, never florid, and, above all, never has any ostentation of cleverness. The beauty of Claude's work is not to be sought primarily in his drawing: it is not a beauty of expressive parts but the beauty of a whole. It corresponds in fact to the poetry of his century—to Milton or Racine. It is in the cumulative effect of the perfect co-ordination of parts none of which is by itself capable of absorbing our attention or fascinating our imagination that the power of a picture by Claude lies. It is the unity and not the content that affects us. There is, of course, content, but the content is only adequate to its purpose and never claims our attention on its own account. The objects he presents to us have no claim on him but as parts of a scheme. They have no life and purpose of their own, and for that very reason it is right that they should be stated in vague and general terms. He wishes a tree to convey to the eye only what the word " tree " might suggest at once to the inner vision. We think first of the mass of waving shade held up against the brilliance of the sky, and this, even with all his detailed elaboration, is about where Claude, whether by good fortune or design, leaves us. It is the same with his rocks, his water, his animals. They are all made for the mental imagery of the contemplative wanderer, not of the acute and ardent observer. But where Claude is supreme is in the marvellous invention with which he combines and recombines these abstract symbols so as to arouse in us more purely than nature herself can the mood of pastoral delight. That Claude was deeply influenced by Virgil one would naturally suppose from his antiquarian classicism, and a drawing in the British Museum shows that he had the idea of illustrating the Æneid. In any case his pictures translate into the language of painting much of the sentiment of Virgil's Eclogues, and that with a purity and grace that rival his original. In his landscapes Melibœus always leaves his goats to repose with Daphnis under the murmuring shade, waiting till his herds come of themselves to drink at the ford, or in sadder moods of passionless regret one hears the last murmurs of the lament for Gallus as the well-pastured goats turn homewards beneath the evening star.

Claude is the most ardent worshipper that ever was of the *genius loci*. Of his landscapes one always feels that " some god is in this place." Never, it is true, one of the greater gods: no mysterious and fearful Pan, no soul-stirring Bacchus or all-embracing Demeter; scarcely, though he tried more than once deliberately to invoke them, Apollo and the Muses, but some mild local deity, the inhabitant of a rustic shrine whose presence only heightens the glamour of the scene.

It is the sincerity of this worship, and the purity and directness of its expression, which makes the lover of landscape turn with such constant affection to Claude, and the chief means by which he communicates it is the unity and perfection of his general design; it is not by form considered in itself, but by the planning of his tone divisions, that he appeals, and here, at least, he is a past master. This splendid architecture of the tone masses is, indeed, the really great quality in his pictures; its perfection and solidity are what enables them to bear the weight of so meticulous and, to our minds, tiresome an elaboration of detail without loss of unity, and enables us even to accept the enamelled hardness and tightness of his surface. But many people of to-day, accustomed to our more elliptical and quick-witted modes of expression, are so impatient of these qualities that they can only appreciate Claude's greatness through the medium of his drawings, where the general skeleton of the design is seen without its adornments, and in a medium which he used with perfect ease and undeniable beauty. Thus to reject the pictures is, I think, an error, because it was only when a design had been exposed to constant correction and purification that Claude got out of it its utmost expressiveness, and his improvisations steadily grow under his critical revision, to their full perfection. But in the drawings, at all events, Claude's great powers of design are readily seen, and the study of the drawings has this advantage also, that through them we come to know of a Claude whose existence we could never have suspected by examining only his finished pictures.

In speaking of the drawings it is well to recognise that they fall into different classes with different purposes and aims. We need not, for instance, here consider the records of finished compositions in the " Liber Veritatis." There remain designs for paintings in all stages of completeness, from the first suggestive idea to the finished cartoon and the drawings from nature. It is, perhaps, scarcely necessary to remark that it would have been quite foreign to Claude's conception of his art to have painted a picture from nature. He, himself, clearly distinguished sharply between his studies and his compositions. His studies, therefore, were not incipient pictures, but exercises done for his own pleasure or for the fertility they gave to his subsequent invention, and they have the unchecked spontaneity and freedom of hand that one would expect in such unreflecting work. These studies again fall into two groups: first, studies of detail, generally of foliage or of tree forms, and occasionally of rocks and flowers; and secondly, studies of general effects. Of the studies of detail I have already said something. They have the charm of an easy and distinguished calligraphy, and of a refined selection of the decorative possibilities of the things seen, but without any of that penetrating investigation of their vital nature which gives its chief beauty to the best work of this kind.

It is, indeed, in the second group of studies from nature that we come from time to time upon motives that startle and surprise us. We find in these a susceptibility to natural charms which, in its width of range and freedom from the traditional limitations of the art of landscape, is most remarkable. Here we find not only Claude the prim seventeenth-century classic, but Claude the romanticist, anticipating the chief ideas of Corot's later development,[1] and Claude the impressionist, anticipating Whistler and the discovery of Chinese landscape, as, for instance, in the marvellous *aperçu* of a mist effect, in the British Museum.[2] Or, again, in a view which is quite different from any of these, but quite as remote from the Claude of the oil-paintings, in the great view of the Tiber, a masterpiece of hurried, almost unconscious planning of bold contrasts of transparent gloom and dazzling light on water and plain.

The impression one gets from looking through a collection of Claude's drawings like that at the British Museum is of a man without any keen feeling for objects in themselves, but singularly open to impressions of general effects in nature, watching always for the shifting patterns of foliage and sky to arrange themselves in some beautifully significant pattern and choosing it with fine and critical taste. But at the same time he was a man with vigorous ideas of the laws of design and the necessity of perfectly realised unity, and to this I suppose one must ascribe the curious contrast between the narrow limits of his work in oil as compared with the wide range, the freedom and the profound originality of his work as a draughtsman. Among all these innumerable effects which his ready susceptibility led him to record he found but a few which were capable of being reduced to that logical and mathematical formula which he demanded before complete realisation could be tolerated. In his drawings he composes sometimes with strong diagonal lines,

[1] As, for instance, in a wonderful drawing, "On the Banks of the Tiber," in Mr. Heseltine's collection.

[2] It is not impossible that Claude got the hint for such a treatment as this from the impressionist efforts of Græco-Roman painters. That he studied such works we know from a copy of one by him in the British Museum.

sometimes with free and unstable balance. In his pictures he has recourse to a regular system of polarity, balancing his masses carefully on either side of the centre, sometimes even framing it in like a theatrical scene with two *repoussoirs* pushed in on either side. One must suppose, then, that he approached the composition of his pictures with a certain timidity, that he felt that safety, when working on a large scale, could only be secured by a certain recognised type of structure, so that out of all the various moods of nature to which his sensitive spirit answered only one lent itself to complete expression. One wishes at times that he had tried more. There is in the British Museum a half-effaced drawing on blue paper, an idea for treating the *Noli me tangere* which, had he worked it out, would have added to his complete mastery of bucolic landscape a masterpiece of what one may call tragic landscape. It is true that here, as elsewhere, the figures are in themselves totally inadequate, but they suggested an unusual and intense key to the landscape. On the outskirts of a dimly suggested wood the figures meet and hold converse; to the right the mound of Calvary glimmers pale and ghostlike against the night sky, while over the distant city the first pink flush of dawn begins. It is an intensely poetical conception. Claude has here created a landscape in harmony with deeper, more mystical aspirations than elsewhere, and, had he given free rein to his sensibilities, we should look to him even more than we do now as the greatest inventor of the motives of pure landscape. As it is, the only ideas to which he gave complete though constantly varied expression are those of pastoral repose.

Claude's view of landscape is false to nature in that it is entirely anthropocentric. His trees exist for pleasant shade; his peasants to give us the illusion of pastoral life, not to toil for a living. His world is not to be lived in, only to be looked at in a mood of pleasing melancholy or suave reverie. It is, therefore as true to one aspect of human desire, as it is false to the facts of life. It may be admitted that this is not the finest kind of art—it is the art of a self-centred and refined luxury which looks on nature as a garden to its own pleasure-house—but few will deny its genial and moderating charm, and few of us live so strenuously as never to feel a sense of nostalgia for that Saturnian reign to which Virgil and Claude can waft us.

AUBREY BEARDSLEY'S DRAWINGS[1]

MESSRS. CARFAX have on view the most complete collection of Beardsley's drawings that has hitherto been shown. The development of his precocious and eccentric genius can here be studied in typical examples. We have the drawings of his childhood—drawings inspired by Dicky Doyle and Robida, but in which is already apparent his proclivity to the expression of moral depravity. We pass at a leap from these crude and artistically feeble works to the astonishing " Siegfried," in which he is already a complete and assured master of an entirely personal style.

From this time onwards, for the remaining six years of his life, Beardsley kept on producing with the fertility of those artists whom the presage of an early death stimulates to a desperate activity. His style was constantly changing in accidentals, but always the same in essentials. He was a confirmed eclectic, borrowing from all ages and all countries. And true eclectic and genuine artist as he was, he converted all his borrowings to his own purposes. It mattered nothing what he fed on; the strange and perverse economy of his nature converted the food into a poison. His line is based

[1] Athenæum, 1904.

upon that of Antonio Pollajuolo. Again and again
in his drawings of the nude we see how carefully he
must have copied that master of structural and nervous
line. But he uses it for something quite other than
its original purpose; he converts it from a line expressive
of muscular tension and virile force into one expressive
of corruption and decay. Mantegna, too, was a favourite
with Beardsley, who seems to have had a kind of craving
for the opposites to his own predominant qualities;
and from Mantegna, the most austere of Italians, he
derived again and again motives for his illustrations
of depravity. The eighteenth century, China, Japan,
even the purest Greek art, were all pressed into his
service; the only thing he could do nothing with was
nature itself. Here he was entirely at a loss, and whenever he yielded to the pressure of contemporary fashions
and attempted to record impressions of things seen,
as in the topical illustrations of plays which he contri-
buted to the *Pall Mall Magazine*, he failed to be even
mediocre. Everything that was to be in the least expressive had to come entirely from within, from the night-
mares of his own imagination.

His amazing gift of hand is perhaps the quality
which most .obviously attracts attention, the quality
which endeared him most to publishers and process-
block makers. It was the one indisputable quality
he possessed, not to be denied by the most adverse
critic, and yet in itself it is no more than thousands
of journeymen artists—engravers, die-cutters, and such
like—have always possessed. Nor, to be perfectly
frank, is the quality of his line of a very high order;
its precision is not unfrequently mechanical. Whistler
called him the last of the writing-masters, and there
was a truth in this, if we may add that the style of
writing which he favoured was degenerate. His long,
meandering flourishes ending in sharp spikes and dots,
however firm and precise the line, are often mean in

intention and poor in quality. What is deserving of real admiration is the fertility of his invention, the skill with which he finds the formula which corresponds, in his peculiar language, with what he wants to describe. As an instance, one may take the garden background to the " Platonic Lament " in the Salome series, where the rose trellis and cut yew-tree behind are brilliant examples of this kind of epitomized description. Still more important artistically, and closely connected with this power of invention, is the real beauty of his spacing, the admirable planning of masses of black and white. At times, as in the " Dancer's Reward," he rises almost to the height of the great Greek vase-painters in this respect, though, if we look even at this in detail, the line has an intricacy, a *mesquinerie*, which is the very opposite of the Greek ideal of draughtsmanship.

No less remarkable is his success in the decorative planning of three tones, of black, white, and grey, and he divides these with such subtle skill that for once it is not a mere false analogy to talk of the colour effect of designs in black and white; for he so disposes the three tones, getting the grey by an evenly distributed network of fine black lines, that each tone produces the sensation of something as distinct from the others as do flat washes of different tints. The " Frontispiece to Salome " is an excellent example of this.

Beardsley had, then, in an extraordinary degree, the decorative impulse, the motive which made the mediæval scribe flourish his pen all over the margins of his vellum page; and, spurred by this impulse, he had the patience of an Indian craftsman, covering whole sheets with minute dots and scarcely perceptible lines. This instinct in its purest form rarely makes for the finest art; it is only when controlled by a larger, more genial sentiment for architectural mass that it becomes ennobled, and with Beardsley in spite of the bold oppositions of his blacks and whites, in spite of his occasional wilful simplification, this rarely occurred. One might even argue that to some extent Beardsley's moral perversity actually prevented him, in spite of his extraordinary specific talent for design, from ever becoming a great designer. It was just this *mesquinerie* of line, this littleness and intricacy of the mere decorator, this love of elegance rather than beauty, which on purely artistic grounds one finds to be his great failing, that he cherished as a means of expressing his diabolism. But if Beardsley was corrupt, he was certainly sincere in his corruption. There is no suggestion in his work, as in that of some modern artists, like Señor Zuloaga, that corruption is an affectation taken up in order to astonish the *bourgeoisie*. Beardsley is never funny or amusing or witty; his attempts in this direction are contemptible; still less is he voluptuous or seductive; he is very serious, very much in earnest. There is even a touch of hieratic austerity and pomp in his style, as becomes the arch-priest of a Satanic cultus. He has, indeed, all the stigmata of the religious artist —the love of pure decoration, the patient elaboration and enrichment of surface, the predilection for flat tones and precision of contour, the want of the sense of mass and relief, the extravagant richness of invention. It is as the Fra Angelico of Satanism that his work will always have an interest for those who are curious about this recurrent phase of complex civilisations. But if we are right in our analysis of his work, the finest qualities of design can never be appropriated to the expression of such morbid and perverted ideals; nobility and geniality of design are attained only by those who, whatever their actual temperament, cherish these qualities in their imagination.

THE FRENCH POST-IMPRESSIONISTS[1]

When the first Post-Impressionist Exhibition was held in these Galleries two years ago the English public became for the first time fully aware of the existence of a new movement in art, a movement which was the more disconcerting in that it was no mere variation upon accepted themes but implied a reconsideration of the very purpose and aim as well as the methods of pictorial and plastic art. It was not surprising, therefore, that a public which had come to admire above everything in a picture the skill with which the artist produced illusion should have resented an art in which such skill was completely subordinated to the direct expression of feeling. Accusations of clumsiness and incapacity were freely made, even against so singularly accomplished an artist as Cézanne. Such darts, however, fall wide of the mark, since it is not the object of these artists to exhibit their skill or proclaim their knowledge, but only to attempt to express by pictorial and plastic form certain spiritual experiences; and in conveying these, ostentation of skill is likely to be even more fatal than downright incapacity.

Indeed, one may fairly admit that the accusation of want of skill and knowledge, while ridiculous in the case of Cézanne is perfectly justified as regards one artist represented—for the first time in England—in the present Exhibition, namely, Rousseau. Rousseau was a custom-house officer who painted without any training in the art. His pretensions to paint made him the butt of a great deal of ironic wit, but scarcely any one now would deny the authentic quality of his

[1] Preface to Catalogue of second Post-Impressionist Exhibition, Grafton Galleries, 1912.

inspiration or the certainty of his imaginative conviction. Here then is one case where want of skill and knowledge do not completely obscure, though they may mar, expression. And this is true of all perfectly naïve and primitive art. But most of the art here seen is neither naïve nor primitive. It is the work of highly civilised and modern men trying to find a pictorial language appropriate to the sensibilities of the modern outlook.

Another charge that is frequently made against these artists is that they allow what is merely capricious, or even what is extravagant and eccentric, in their work —that it is not serious, but an attempt to impose on the good-natured tolerance of the public. This charge of insincerity and extravagance is invariably made against any new manifestation of creative art. It does not of course follow that it is always wrong. The desire to impose by such means certainly occurs, and is sometimes temporarily successful. But the feeling on the part of the public may, and I think in this case does, arise from a simple misunderstanding of what these artists set out to do. The difficulty springs from a deep-rooted conviction due to long-established custom, that the aim of painting is the descriptive imitation of natural forms. Now, these artists do not seek to give what can, after all, be but a pale reflex of actual appearance, but to arouse the conviction of a new and definite reality. They do not seek to imitate form, but to create form; not to imitate life, but to find an equivalent for life. By that I mean that they wish to make images which by the clearness of their logical structure, and by their closely-knit unity of texture, shall appeal to our disinterested and contemplative imagination with something of the same vividness as the things of actual life appeal to our practical activities. In fact, they aim not at illusion but at reality.

The logical extreme of such a method would undoubtedly be the attempt to give up all resemblance to natural form, and to create a purely abstract language of form—a visual music; and the later works of Picasso show this clearly enough. They may or may not be successful in their attempt. It is too early to be dogmatic on the point, which can only be decided when our sensibilities to such abstract forms have been more practised than they are at present. But I would suggest that there is nothing ridiculous in the attempt to do this. Such a picture as Picasso's "Head of a Man" would undoubtedly be ridiculous if, having set out to make a direct imitation of the actual model, he had been incapable of getting a better likeness. But Picasso did nothing of the sort. He has shown in his "Portrait of Mlle. L. B." that he could so do at least as well as any one if he wished, but he is here attempting to do something quite different.

No such extreme abstraction marks the work of Matisse. The actual objects which stimulated his creative invention are recognisable enough. But here, too, it is an equivalence, not a likeness, of nature that is sought. In opposition to Picasso, who is pre-eminently plastic, Matisse aims at convincing us of the reality of his forms by the continuity and flow of his rhythmic line by the logic of his space relations, and, above all, by an entirely new use of colour. In this, as in his markedly rhythmic design, he approaches more than any other European to the ideals of Chinese art. His work has to an extraordinary degree that decorative unity of design which distinguishes all the artists of this school.

Between these two extremes we may find ranged almost all the remaining artists. On the whole the influence of Picasso on the younger men is more evident than that of Matisse. With the exception of Braque none of them push their attempts at abstraction of form so far as Picasso, but simplification along these lines is apparent in the work of Derain, Herbin, Marchand,

and L'Hote. Other artists, such as Doucet and Asselin, are content with the ideas of simplification of form as existing in the general tradition of the Post-Impressionist movement, and instead of feeling for new methods of expression devote themselves to expressing what is most poignant and moving in contemporary life. But however various the directions in which different groups are exploring the newly-formed regions of expressive form they all alike derive in some measure from the great originator of the whole idea, Cézanne. And since one must always refer to him to understand the origin of these ideas, it has been thought well to include a few examples of his work in the present Exhibition, although this year it is mainly the moderns, and not the old masters that are represented. To some extent, also, the absence of the earlier masters in the exhibition itself is made up for by the retrospective exhibition of Monsieur Druet's admirable photographs. Here Cézanne, Gauguin, and Van Gogh can be studied at least in the main phases of their development.

Finally, I should like to call attention to a distinguishing characteristic of the French artists seen here, namely, the markedly Classic spirit of their work. This will be noted as distinguishing them to some extent from the English, even more perhaps from the Russians, and most of all from the great mass of modern painting in every country. I do not mean by Classic, dull, pedantic, traditional, reserved, or any of those similar things which the word is often made to imply. Still less do I mean by calling them Classic that they paint "Visits to Æsculapius" or "Nero at the Colosseum." I mean that they do not rely for their effect upon associated ideas, as I believe Romantic and Realistic artists invariably do.

All art depends upon cutting off the practical responses to sensations of ordinary life, thereby setting free a pure and as it were disembodied functioning of the spirit; but in so far as the artist relies on the associated ideas of the objects which he represents, his work is not completely free and pure, since romantic associations imply at least an imagined practical activity. The disadvantage of such an art of associated ideas is that its effect really depends on what we bring with us: it adds no entirely new factor to our experience. Consequently, when the first shock of wonder or delight is exhausted the work produces an ever lessening reaction. Classic art, on the other hand, records a positive and disinterestedly passionate state of mind. It communicates a new and otherwise unattainable experience. Its effect, therefore, is likely to increase with familiarity. Such a classic spirit is common to the best French work of all periods from the twelfth century onwards, and though no one could find direct reminiscences of a Nicholas Poussin here, his spirit seems to revive in the work of artists like Derain. It is natural enough that the intensity and singleness of aim with which these artists yield themselves to certain experiences in the face of nature may make their work appear odd to those who have not the habit of contemplative vision, but it would be rash for us, who as a nation are in the habit of treating our emotions, especially our æsthetic emotions, with a certain levity, to accuse them of caprice or insincerity. It is because of this classic concentration of feeling (which by no means implies abandonment) that the French merit our serious attention. It is this that makes their art so difficult on a first approach but gives it its lasting hold on the imagination.

NOTE.—At least one French artist of great merit was unrepresented at the Post-Impressionist Exhibitions—Georges Rouault, a fellow-pupil with Matisse of Gustave Moreau. He stands alone in the movement as being a visionary, though, unlike most visionaries, his expression is based on a profound knowledge of natural appearances.

DRAWINGS AT THE BURLINGTON FINE ARTS CLUB[1]

THE Burlington Fine Arts Club have arranged a most interesting collection of drawings by dead masters. Abandoning the club's usual method of taking a particular period or country, the committee have this time allowed their choice to range over many periods and countries, excluding only living artists, and admitting one so recently dead as Degas. This variety of material naturally stimulates one to hazard some general speculations on the nature of drawing as an art. "H. T.," who writes the preface to the catalogue, already points the way in this direction by some *obiter dicta*. He points out that the essence of drawing is not the line, but its content. He says:

A single line may mean nothing beyond a line; add another alongside and both disappear, and we are aware only of the contents, and a form is expressed. The beauty of a line is in its result in the form which it helps to bring into being.

Here the author has undoubtedly pointed out the most essential quality of good drawing. I should dispute, rather by way of excessive caution, his first statement, "A single line may mean nothing beyond a line," since a line is always at its least the record of a gesture, indicating a good deal about its maker's personality, his tastes and even probably the period when he lived; but I entirely agree that the main point is always the effect which two lines have of evoking the idea of a certain volume having a certain form. When "H.T." adds that "Draughtsmen know this, but writers on art do not seem to," he seems to be too sweeping. Even so bad a writer on art as Pliny had picked up the

[1] Burlington Magazine, 1912.

idea from a Greek art critic, for in describing the drawing of Parrhasios he says: [1]

> By the admission of artists he was supreme in contour. This is the last subtlety of painting; for to paint the main body and centres of objects is indeed something of an achievement, but one in which many have been famous, but to paint the edges of bodies and express the disappearing planes is rare in the history of art. For the contour must go round itself and so end that it promises other things behind and shows that which it hides.

This is an admirable account, since it gives the clue to the distinction between descriptive drawing and drawing in which the contour does not arrest the form, but creates plastic relief of the whole enclosed volume. Now, this plastic drawing can never be attained by a mere *description* of the edges of objects. Such a description, however exact, can at the utmost do no more than recall vividly the original object; it cannot enable the spectator to realise its plastic volume more clearly than the original object would. Now, when we look at a really good drawing we do get a much more vivid sense of a plastic volume than we get from actual objects.

Unfortunately this is a very severe test to apply, and would, I think, relegate to an inferior class the vast majority of drawings, even of those in the present exhibition. The vast majority of drawings even by the celebrated masters do appeal mainly by other more

---

[1] I have had to paraphrase this passage, but add the original. Whether my paraphrase is correct in detail or not, I think there can be little doubt about the general meaning.

Plin., *Nat. Hist.*, xxxv. 67: "Parrhasius . . . confessione artificium in liniis extremis palmam adeptus. Hæc est picturæ summa sublimitas; corpora enim pingere et media rerum est quidem magni operis, sed in quo multi gloriam tulerint. Extrema corporum facere et desinentis picturæ modum includere rarum in successu artis invenitur. Ambire enim debet se extremitas ipsa, et sic desinere ut promittat alia post se ostendatque etiam quae occultat."

subsidiary qualities, by the brightness of their descriptive power, and by the elegance and facility of their execution. There is an undoubted pleasure in the contemplation of mere skill, and there are few ways of demonstrating sheer skill of hand more convincingly than the drawing of a complex series of curves with perfect exactitude and great rapidity. And when the curves thus brilliantly drawn describe vividly some object in life towards which we have pleasing associations we get a complex pleasure which is only too likely to be regarded as an æsthetic experience when in fact it is nothing of the kind.

The author of the preface has quite clearly seen that this element of brilliance in the execution of the line does frequently come into play, and he considers this calligraphic quality to be always a sign of a lowered æsthetic purpose, citing Tiepolo quite rightly as a great master of such qualities. And he quite rightly points out that with the deliberate pursuit of calligraphy there is always a tendency to substitute type forms for individual forms. On the other hand, all good drawing also tends to create types, since a type results from the synthetic unity of the design. The real question here would seem to be the fulness or emptiness of the type created, and it would be fair to say that the calligraphic draughtsman accepted most readily an empty type. For instance, one would have to admit that Ingres created a type, and repeated it as much as Tiepolo, only Ingres continually generated his type of form upon actual material, whereas Tiepolo tended merely to repeat his without enriching it with fresh material.

The Exhibition has been to some extent arranged around Ingres, and as many of his drawings as possible have been collected. Ingres has long been accepted in the schools as *par excellence* the great modern master of drawing. His great saying, "*Le dessin c'est la probité de l'art*," has indeed become a watchword of the schools, and an excuse for indulgence in a great deal of gratuitous and misplaced moral feeling. It has led to the display of all kinds of pedagogic folly. Art is a passion or it is nothing. It is certainly a very bad moral gymnasium. It is useless to try to make a kind of moral parallel bars out of the art of drawing. You will certainly spoil the drawing, and it is doubtful if you will get the morals. Drawing is a passion to the draughtsman just as much as colour is to the colourist, and the draughtsman has no reason to feel moral superiority because of the nature of his passion. He is fortunate to have it, and there is an end of the matter. Ingres himself had the passion for draughtsmanship very intensely, though perhaps one would scarcely guess it from the specimens shown in this exhibition. These unfortunately are, with few exceptions, taken from that large class of drawings which he did as a young man in Rome. He was already married, and was poor. He was engaged on some of his biggest and most important compositions, on which he was determined to spare no pains or labour; consequently he found himself forced to earn his living by doing these brilliant and minutely accurate portraits of the aristocratic tourists and their families, who happened to pass through Rome. These drawings bear the unmistakable mark of their origins. They are commissions, and they are done to satisfy the sitter. Anything like serious research for form is out of the question; there is little here but Ingres's extreme facility and a certain negative good taste. Probably the only drawing here which shows Ingres's more serious powers is the tight, elaborate and rather repellent study for the "Apotheosis of Napoleon," which is a splendid discovery of composition within a round. But the real fact is, I believe, that Ingres's power as a draughtsman hardly ever comes out fully in his drawings; one must turn to his paintings to see how great and sincere a researcher he was. In his drawings he was too much preoccupied with the perfect description of facts; when he came to the painting he began that endless process of readjustment and balance of contours which make him so great and original a designer. If one places his drawings and studies from the nude for, say, his "Venus Anadyomene" beside the photograph of the picture one gets some idea of the tireless and passionate research for the exact correspondence of the contours on either side of the figure which Ingres undertook. He throws over one by one all the brilliant notations of natural form in the studies, and arrives bit by bit at an intensely abstract and simplified statement of the general relations. But though the new statement is emptied of its factual content, it has now become far more compact, far more intense in its plasticity. Here and there among Ingres's innumerable drawings one may find a nude study in which already this process of elimination and balance has taken place, but the examples are rare, and if one would understand why Ingres is one of the great masters of design, one must face the slightly repellent quality of his oil paintings rather than allow oneself to be seduced by the elegance and ease of his drawings.

It would, I think, be possible to show that very few great designers have attained to full expression in line. I suspect, indeed, that the whole tradition of art in Europe, since about the end of the fifteenth century, has been against such complete expression. If we compare the great masterpieces of pure drawings such as the drawings of figures on Persian pots of the twelfth and thirteenth centuries, and the few remaining examples of drawings by the Italian primitives of the fourteenth and early fifteenth centuries, with the vast mass of European drawings subsequent to that date, we see, I think, the contrast of aims and purpose of the two groups. Somewhere about the time of Filippino Lippi there was formulated an idea of drawing which has more or less held the field ever since in art schools.

As most drawing has centred in the human figure we may describe it in relation to that, the more so that this view of drawing undoubtedly came in with the study of anatomy. The general principle is that there are certain cardinal facts about the figure, or points of cardinal importance in the rendering of structure—the artist is trained to observe these with special care, since they become the *points de repère* for his drawing. And since they are thus specially observed they are noted with a special accent. When once the artist has learned to grasp the relations of these *points de repère* firmly he learns also to pass from one to the other with great ease and rapidity, not to say with a certain indifference as to what happens in the passage. By this method the essentials of structure and movement of a figure are accurately given and the whole statement can be made with that easy facility and rapidity of line which gives a peculiar pleasure. Such drawing has the merit of being at once structurally accurate and more or less calligraphically pleasing. The most admired masters, such as Vandyke, Watteau, even to some extent Rubens, all exhibit the characteristics of such a conception. Now in the earlier kind of drawing there were no recognised *points de repère*, no particular moments of emphasis; the line was so drawn that at every point its relation to the opposed contour was equally close, the tension so to speak was always across the line and not along its direction. The essential thing was the position of the line, not its quality, so that there was the less inclination to aim at that easy rapidity which marks the later draughtsmanship. Essentially, then, this earlier drawing was less descriptive and more purely evocative of form. It may well be that the demands made upon the artist by the closer study of nature brought in by the

Renaissance became an almost insuperable barrier to artists in the attempt to find any such completely synthetic vision of form as lay to hand for their predecessors. We see, for instance, in Albert Dürer's "Beetle" an example of purely descriptive and analytic drawing with no attempt at inner coherence of form. On the other hand, of course, all the great formalists made deliberate efforts to come through the complex of phenomena to some abstract synthesis. Fra Bartolomeo and Raphael clearly made such abstraction a matter of deliberate study, but as I have pointed out in the case of Ingres, the obsession of fact has generally forced the artist to such a long series of experiments towards the final synthetic form that it is only in the finished picture that it emerges fully.

On the other hand, some modern masters have also found their way through, more or less completely, and from this point of view few drawings in the exhibition are as remarkable as the drawing of a seated woman by Corot. Here one supposes it may be a kind of *naïveté* of vision rather than the exhaustive process of an Ingres, that has led Corot to this vividly realised plasticity of form. I find the essentials of good drawing more completely realised here than in almost any other drawing in the exhibition, and yet how little of a professional draughtsman Corot was. It is hard to speak here of Degas's works as drawings. With one exception they are pastels and essentially paintings, but they are of great beauty and show him victorious over his own formidable cleverness, his unrivalled but dangerous power of witty notation.

At the opposite pole to Corot's drawing with its splendid revelation of plastic significance we must put Menzel with his fussy preoccupation with undigested fact. It is hard indeed to see quite how Menzel's drawings found their way into this good company, except perhaps as drunken helots, for they are conspicuously devoid of any æsthetic quality whatever. They are without any rhythmic unity, without any glimmering of a sense of style, and style though it be as cheap as Rowlandson's is still victorious over sheer misinformed literalness. Somewhere between Menzel and Corot we must place Charles Keane, and I fear, in spite of the rather exaggerated claims made for him in the preface, he is nearer to Menzel, though even so, how much better! The early Millais drawing is of course an astounding attempt by a man of prodigious gift and no sensibility to pretend that he had the latter. It is a pity there are no Rossettis here to show the authentic inspiration of which this is the echo.

I come now to the Rembrandts, of which there are several good examples. Rembrandt always intrigues one by the multiplicity and diversity of his gifts and the struggle between his profound imaginative insight and his excessive talents. The fact is, I believe that Rembrandt was never a linealist, that he never had the conception of contour clearly present to him. He was too intensely and too inveterately a painter and a chiaroscurist. The last thing he saw was a contour, and more than anything else it eluded his vision. His vision was in fact so intensely fixed on the interplay of planes, their modulation into one another, and on the balance of directions, that with him the drawn line has a quite peculiar and personal meaning. It is used first to indicate directions of stress and movement, as, for instance, a straight line will be dashed down to indicate, not the contour of a limb, but its direction, the line along which stress of action takes place. He seems almost to dread the contour, to prefer to make strokes either inside or outside of it, and to trust to the imagination to discover its whereabouts, anything rather than a final definite statement which would arrest the interplay of planes. The line is also used to suggest very vaguely and tentatively the division of planes;

but almost always when he comes to use wash on top of the line his washes go across the lines, so that here too one can hardly say the line indicates the division so much as the approximate position of a plane.

In conclusion I would suggest that the art of pure contour is comparatively rare in modern art. For what I should cite as great and convincing examples of that art I would ask the reader to turn to the "Morgan Byzantine Enamels" (*Burlington Magazine*, vol. xxi. pp. 3, 65, 127, 219, 290), the "Manafi-i-Heiwan" (*Burl. Mag.*, vol. xxiii. pp. 224, 261), and to Vignier, "Persian Pottery" (*Burl. Mag.*, vol. xxv. p. 211), while other examples might be found among Byzantine and Carolingian miniaturists.

Now, this art depends upon a peculiarly synthetic vision and a peculiar system of distortion, without which the outline would arrest the movement of planes too definitely. There indeed is the whole crux of the art of line drawing; the line generates a volume, but it also arrests the planes too definitely: that is why in some great modern artists, as we saw in the case of Rembrandt, there is a peculiar kind of dread of the actual contour. It is felt by those who are sensitive to the interplay and movement of planes that the line must in some way, by its quality or its position, or by breaks or repetitions, avoid arresting the imagination by too positive a statement. It was almost a peculiarity of the early art that I have cited that it was able to express a form in a quite complete, evenly drawn contour without this terrible negative effect of the line. I say almost a peculiarity, because I think a few quite modern artists, such as Matisse and perhaps Modigliani, have recovered such a power, but in the great mass of post-Renaissance drawing the art of the pure contour in line has broken down, and the essential qualities even of the great linealists are only to be seen fully in their paintings; the drawn line itself has had to take on other functions.

PAUL CÉZANNE[1]

IN a society which is as indifferent to works of art as our modern industrialism it seems paradoxical that artists of all kinds should loom so large in the general consciousness of mankind—that they should be remembered with reverence and boasted of as national assets when statesmen, lawyers, and soldiers are forgotten. The great mass of modern men could rub along happily enough without works of art or at least without new ones, but society would be sensibly more bored if the artist died out altogether. The fact is that every honest bourgeois, however sedate and correct his life, keeps a hidden and scarce-admitted yearning for that other life of complete individualism which hard necessity or the desire for success has denied him. In contemplating the artist he tastes vicariously these forbidden joys. He regards the artist as a strange species, half idiot, half divine, but above all irresponsibly and irredeemably himself. He seems equally strange in his outrageous egoism and his superb devotion to an idea.

Also in a world where the individual is squeezed and moulded and polished by the pressure of his fellow-men the artist remains irreclaimably individual—in a world where every one else is being perpetually educated the artist remains ineducable—where others are shaped, he grows. Cézanne realised the type of the artist in its purest, most unmitigated form, and M. Vollard has had the wit to write a book about Cézanne and not about Cézanne's pictures. The time may come when we shall require a complete study of Cézanne's work, a measured judgment of his achievement and

[1] Burlington Magazine, 1917: "Paul Cézanne," by Ambroise Vollard (Paris, 1915).

position—it would probably be rash to attempt it as yet. Meanwhile we have M. Vollard's portrait, at once documented and captivating. Should the book ever become as well known as it deserves there would be, one guesses, ten people fascinated by Cézanne for one who would walk down the street to see his pictures.

The art historian may sometimes regret that Vasari did not give us more of the æsthetics of his time; but Vasari knew his business, knew, perhaps, that the æsthetics of an age are quickly superseded but that the human document remains of perennial interest to mankind. M. Vollard has played Vasari to Cézanne and done so with the same directness and simplicity, the same narrative ease, the same insatiable delight in the oddities and idiosyncrasies of his subject. And what a model he had to paint ! Every word and every gesture he records sticks out with the rugged relief of a character in which everything is due to the compulsion of inner forces, in which nothing has been planed down or smoothed away by external pressure—not that external pressure was absent but that the inner compulsion—the inevitable bent of Cézanne's temperament, was irresistible. In one very important detail Cézanne was spared by life—he always had enough to live on. The thought of a Cézanne having to earn his living is altogether too tragic. But if life spared him in this respect his temperament spared him nothing —for this rough Provençal countryman had so exasperated a sensibility that the smallest detail of daily life, the barking of a dog, the noise of a lift in a neighbouring house, the dread of being touched even by his own son might produce at any moment a nervous explosion. At such times his first relief was in cursing and swearing, but if this failed the chances were that his anger vented itself on his pictures—he would cut one to pieces with his palette knife, or failing that roll

it up and throw it into the stove. M. Vollard describes
with delightful humour the tortures he endured in the
innumerable sittings which he gave Cézanne for his
portrait—with what care he avoided any subject of
conversation which might lead to misunderstanding.
But with all his adroitness there were one or two crises
in which the portrait was threatened with the dreaded
knife—fortunately Cézanne always found some other
work on which to vent his indignation, and the portrait survived, though after a hundred and fifteen sittings,
in which Cézanne exacted the immobility of an apple,
the portrait was left incomplete. "I am not displeased
with the shirt front," was Cézanne's characteristic
appreciation.

Two phrases continually recur in Cézanne's conversation which show his curious idiosyncrasies. One
the often-quoted one of his dread that any one
might *"lui jeter le grappin dessus"* and the other
"moi qui suis faible dans la vie." They express his
constant attitude of distrust of his kind—for him
all women were *"des veaux et des calculatrices"*—his
dread of any possible invasion of his personality,
and his sense of impotence in face of the forces of
life.

None the less, though he pathetically exaggerated
his weakness he never seems to have had the least
doubt about his supreme greatness as an artist; what
troubled and irritated him was his incapacity to express
his "sensation" in such terms as would make its
meaning evident to the world. It was for this reason
that he struggled so obstinately and hopelessly to
get into the "Salon de M. Bougereau." His attitude to
conventional art was a strange mixture of admiration
at its skill and of an overwhelming horror of its emptiness—of its so "horrible resemblence."

That fact is that Cézanne had accepted uncritically
all the conventions in the pathetic belief that it was

the olny way of safety for one "so feeble in life." So
he continued to believe in the Catholic Church not
from any religious conviction but because "Rome
was so strong"—so, too, he believed in the power
and importance of the "Salon de Bougereau" which
he hated as much as he feared. So, too, with what
seems a paradoxical humility he let it be known, when
his fame had already been established among the intelligent, that he would be glad to have the Legion of
Honour. But here, too, he was destined to fail. The
weighty influence and distinguished position of his
friends could avail nothing against the undisguised
horror with which any official heard the dreaded name
of Cézanne. And it appeared that Cézanne was the only
artist in France for whom this distinction was inacces-
sible, even through "influence." Nothing is stranger
in his life than the contrast between the idea the public
formed of Cézanne and the reality. He was one of
those men destined to give rise to a legend which
completely obscured the reality. He was spoken of
as the most violent of revolutionaries—Communard
and Anarchist were the favourite epithets—and all
the time he was a timid little country gentleman of
immaculate respectability who subscribed whole-
heartedly to any reactionary opinion which might
establish his "soundness." He was a timid man who
really believed in only one thing, "his little sensation";
who laboured incessantly to express this peculiar
quality and who had not the faintest notion of doing
anything that could shock the feelings of any mortal
man or woman. No wonder then that when he looked
up from his work and surveyed the world with his
troubled and imperfect intellectual vision he was amazed
and perturbed at the violent antagonism which he had
all unconsciously provoked. No wonder that he became
a shy, distrustful misanthrope, almost incapable of
any association with his kind.

I have suggested that Cézanne was the perfect realisation of the type of the artist—I doubt whether in the whole of Vasari's great picture gallery there is a more complete type of "original." But in order to accept this we must banish from our mind the conventional idea of the artist as a man of flamboyant habit and calculated pose. Nothing is less possible to the real artist than pose—he is less capable of it than the ordinary man of business because more than anyone else his external activities are determined from within by needs and instincts which he himself barely recognises.

On the other hand the imitation artist is a past master of pose, he poses as the sport of natural inclinations whilst he is really deliberately exploiting his caprices; and as he has a natural instinct for the limelight this variety of the "Cabotin" generally manages to sit for the portrait of the artist. Cézanne then, though his external life was of that the most irreproachable of country gentlemen, though he went to mass every Sunday and never willingly left the intimacy of family life, was none the less the purest and most unadulterated of artists, the most narrowly confined to his single activity, the most purely disinterested and the most frankly egoistic of men.

Cézanne had no intellectual independence. I doubt if he had the faintest conception of intellectual truth, but this is not to deny that he had a powerful mind. On the contrary he had a profound intelligence of whatever came within his narrow outlook on life, and above all he had the gift of expression, so that however fantastic, absurd, or naïve his opinions may have been, they were always expressed in such racy and picturesque language that they become interesting as revelations of a very human and genuine personality.

One of the tragi-comedies of Cézanne's life was the story of his early friendship with Zola, followed in middle life by a gradual estrangement, and at last by a total separation. It is perhaps the only blot in M. Vollard's book that he has taken too absolutely Cézanne's point of view, and has hardly done justice to Zola's goodness of heart. The cause of friction, apart from Cézanne's habitual testiness and ill-humour, was that Zola's feeling for art, which had led him in his youth to a heroic championship of the younger men, faded away in middle life. His own practice of literature led him further and further away from any concern with pure art, and he failed to recognise that his own early prophecy of Cézanne's greatness had come true, simply because he himself had become a popular author, and Cézanne had failed of any kind of success. Unfortunately Zola, who had evidently lost all real æsthetic feeling, continued to talk about art, and worse than that he had made the hero of "L'Œuvre" a more or less recognisable portrait of his old friend. Cézanne could not tolerate Zola's gradual acquiescence in worldly ideals and ways of life, and when the Dreyfusard question came up not only did his natural reactionary bias make him a vehement anti-Dreyfusard but he had no comprehension whatever of the heroism of Zola's actions; he found him merely ridiculous, and believed him to be engaged in an ill-conceived scheme of self-advertisement. But for all his contempt of Zola his affection remained deeper than he knew, and when he heard the news of Zola's death Cézanne shut himself up alone in his studio, and was heard sobbing and groaning throughout the day.

Cézanne's is not the only portrait in M. Vollard's entertaining book—there are sketches of many characters, among them the few strange and sympathetic men who appreciated and encouraged Cézanne in his early days. Of Cabaner the musician M. Vollard has collected some charming notes. Cabaner was a "philosopher," and singularly indifferent to the chances of life. During the siege of Paris he met Coppée, and

noticing the shells which were falling he became curious.
"Where do all these bullets come from?" Coppeé:
"It would seem that it is the besiegers who send them."
Cabaner, after a silence: "Is it always the Prussians?"
Coppeé, impatiently: "Who on earth could it be?"
Cabaner: "I don't know . . . other nations!" But
the book is so full of good stories that I must resist
the temptation to quote.

Fortunately M. Vollard has collected also a large
number of Cézanne's *obiter decta* on art. These have
all Cézanne's pregnant wisdom and racy style. They
often contain a whole system of æsthetics in a single
phrase, as, for instance: "What's wanted is to do
Poussin over again from Nature."

They show, moreover, the natural bias of Cézanne's
feelings and their gradual modification as his understanding became more profound. What comes out
clearly, and it must never be forgotten in considering
his art, is that his point of departure was from Roman-
ticism. Delacroix was his god and Ingres, in his early
days, his devil—a devil he learned increasingly to
respect, but one never imagines really to love, "*Ce
Dominique est très fort mais il m'emm——*" That
Cézanne became a supreme master of formal design
every one would nowadays admit, but there is some
excuse for those contemporaries who complained of
his want of drawing. He was not a master of line in
the sense in which Ingres was. "The contour escapes
me," as he said. That is to say he arrived at the contour by a study of the interior planes; he was always
plastic before he was linear. In his early works, such,
for instance, as the "Scene de plein air," he is evidently
inspired by Delacroix; he is almost a romanticist himself in such work, and his design is built upon the contrasts of large and rather loosely drawn silhouettes
of dark and light. In fact it is the method of Tintoretto,
Rubens, and Delacroix.

In the "Bathers resting," painted in 1877, there is already a great change. It is rather by the exact placing of plastic units than by continuous flowing silhouettes that the design holds. Giorgione perhaps, is behind all this, but no longer Tintoretto, and, above all, Poussin has intervened.

In later works, such as the portrait of "Mme. Cézanne in a green-house," the plasticity has become all-important, there is no longer any suggestion of a romantic *decor;* all is reduced to the purest terms of structural design.

These notes on Cézanne's development are prompted by the illustrations in Vollard's book. These are numerous and excellent, and afford a better opportunity for a general study of Cézanne's *œuvre* than any other book. In fact, when the time comes for the complete appreciation of Cézanne, M. Vollard's book will be the most important document existing. It should, however, have a far wider appeal than that. I hope that after the war M. Vollard will bring out a small cheap edition[1]—it should become a classic biography. To say, as I would, that M. Vollard's book is a monument worthy of Cézanne himself is to give it the highest praise.

RENOIR[2]

WHAT a lover of the commonplace Renoir was! It is a rare quality among artists. A theoretically pure artist exists no more than a Euclidean point, but if such a being could exist, every possible actual sight would be equally suitable as a point of departure for his artistic vision. Everything would stir in him the impulse to creation. He would have no predilections,

---

[1] This has been done. "Paul Cézanne," by Ambroise Vollard (Paris).
[2] 1919.

no tastes for this or that kind of thing. In practice every artist is set going by some particular kind of scene in nature, and for the most part artists have to search out some unusual or unexplored aspect of things. Gauguin, for instance, had to go as far as Tahiti. When Renoir heard of this, he said, in a phrase which revealed his own character: "Pourquoi? On peint si bien a Batignolles." But there are plenty of artists who paint more or less well at Batignolles or Bloomsbury and yet are not lovers of the commonplace. Like Walter Sickert, for instance, they find their Tahiti in Mornington Crescent. Though they paint in commonplace surroundings, they generally contrive to catch them at an unexpected angle. Something odd or exotic in their taste for life seems to be normal to artists. The few artists or writers who have shared the tastes of the average man have, as a rule, been like Dickens—to take an obvious case—very imperfect and very impure artists, however great their genius. Among great artists one thinks at once of Rubens as the most remarkable example of a man of common tastes, a lover of all that was rich, exuberant and even florid. Titian, too, comes nearly up to the same standard, except that in youth his whole trend of feeling was distorted by the overpowering influence of Giorgione, whose tastes were recondite and strange. Renoir, in the frankness of his colour harmonies, in his feeling for design and even in the quality of his pigment, constantly reminds us of these two. Now it is easier to see how an artist of the sixteenth or seventeenth century could develop common place tastes than one of our own times. For with the nineteenth century came in a gradual process of differentiation of the artist from the average man. The modern artist finds himself so little understood by the crowd, in his aims and methods, that he tends to become distinct in his whole attitude to life.

What, then, is so peculiar about Renoir is that he has this perfectly ordinary taste in things and yet remains so intensely, so purely, an artist. The fact is perhaps that he was so much an artist that he never had to go round the corner to get his inspiration; the immediate, obvious, front view of everything was more than sufficient to start the creative impulse. He enjoyed instinctively, almost animally, all the common good things of life, and yet he always kept just enough detachment to feel his delight æsthetically—he kept, as it were, just out of reach of appetite.

More than any other great modern artist Renoir trusted implicitly to his own sensibility; he imposed no barrier between his own delight in certain things and the delight which he communicates. He liked passionately the obviously good things of life, the young human animal, sunshine, sky, trees, water, fruit; the things that everyone likes; only he liked them at just the right distance with just enough detachment to replace appetite by emotion. He could rely on this detachment so thoroughly that he could dare, what hardly any] other genuine modern has dared to say how much he liked even a pretty sight. But what gives his art so immediate, so universal an appeal is that his detachment went no further than was just necessary. His sensibility is kept at the exact point where it is transmuted into emotion. And the emotion, though it has of course the generalised æsthetic feeling, keeps something of the fullness and immediacy of the simpler attitude. Not that Renoir was either naïve or stupid. When he chose he showed that he was capable of logical construction and vigorous design. But for his own pleasure he would, as he himself said, have been satisfied to make little isolated records of his delight in the detail of a flower or a lock of hair. With the exception of "Les Parapluies" at the National Gallery we have rarely seen his more deliberate compositions in England. But in all his work alike Renoir remains the man who could trust recklessly his instinctive reaction to life.

Let me confess that these characteristics—this way of keeping, as it were, just out of reach of appetite—makes Renoir to me, personally, a peculiarly difficult artist. My taste for exotic artists such as Cocima Tura and his kin amounts at times to a vice. Consequently, I am sometimes in danger of not doing Renoir justice, because at the first approach to one of his pictures I miss the purely accessory delight of an unexpected attitude. The first approach to one of his pictures may indeed remind one of pictures that would be the delight of the servants' hall, so unaffectedly simple is his acceptances of rosy-cheeked girls, of pretty posies and dappled sunlight. And yet one knows well enough that Renoir was as "artful" as one could wish. Though he had not the biting wit of a Degas, he had a peculiar love of mischievous humour; he was anything but a harmless or innocent character. All his simplicity is on the surface only. The longer one looks, the deeper does Renoir retire behind veil after veil of subtlety. And yet, compared with some modern artists, he was, after all, easy and instinctively simple. Even his plastic unity was arrived at by what seems a more natural method than, say Cézanne's. Whereas Cézanne undertook his indefatigable research for the perspective of the receding planes. Renoir seems to have accepted a very simple general plastic formula. Whatever Cézanne may have meant by his celebrated saying about cones and cylinders, Renoir seems to have thought the sphere and cylinder sufficient for his purpose. The figure presents itself to his eye as an arrangement of more or less hemispherical bosses and cylinders, and he appears generally to arrange the light so that the most prominent part of each boss receives the highest light. From this the planes recede by insensible gradations towards the contour, which generally remains the vaguest, least ascertained part of the modelling. Whatever lies immediately behind the contour tends to become drawn into its sphere of influence, to form an undefined recession enveloping and receiving the receding planes. As the eye passes away from the contour, new but less marked bosses form themselves and fill the background with repetitions of the general theme. The picture tends thus to take the form of a bas-relief in which the recessions are not into the profound distances of pictorial space, but only back, as it were to the block out of which the bossed reliefs emerge, though, of course, by means of atmospheric colour the eye may interpret these recessions as distance. This is clearly in marked contrast to Cézanne's method of suggesting endless recessions of planes with the most complicated interwoven texture.

Renoir's drawing takes on the same fundamental simplicity. An Ingres arrived at the simplified statement necessary for great design by a process of gradual elimination of all the superfluous sinuosities which his hand had recorded in the first drawing from nature. Renoir seems never to have allowed his eye to accept more than the larger elements of mass and direction. His full, rounded curves embrace the form in its most general aspect. With advancing years and continually growing science he was able, at last, to state this essential synthesis with amazing breadth and ease. He continually increased the amplitude of his forms until, in his latest nudes, the whole design is filled with a few perfectly related bosses. Like Titian's, Renoir's power of design increased visibly up to the very end of his life. True, he was capable at all periods of conceiving large and finely co-ordinated compositions, such as "Les Parapluies" and the "Charpentier family"; but at the end even the smallest studies have structural completeness.

A POSSIBLE DOMESTIC ARCHITECTURE[1]

Houses are either builders' houses or architects' houses. Not that speculative builders do not employ architects but they generally employ architects who efface themselves behind the deadly conventionality and bewildering fantasy of their façades. Architects' houses are generally built to the order of a gentleman who wishes his house to have some distinctive character, to stand out from the common herd of houses, either by its greater splendour or its greater discretion. The builders' house, like the dresses of the lower middle class, is generally an imitation of the gentleman's, only of a fashion that has just gone out of date and imitated badly in cheaper materials. No one defends it. It is made so because you must make a house somehow, and bought because it is the usual and therefore inevitable thing. No one enjoys it, no one admires it, it is accepted as part of the use and wont of ordinary life. The gentleman's and the architect's house is different. Here time and thought, and perhaps great ingenuity and taste are employed in giving to the house an individual character. Unfortunately this individual character is generally conscious of its social aspect, of how the house will look, not to those who live in it so much as to those who come to visit. We have no doubt outlived the more vulgar forms of this social consciousness, those which led to the gross display of merely expensive massiveness and profusion. Few modern houses would satisfy Mr. Podsnap. But its subtler forms are still apparent. They generally make themselves felt in the desire to be romantic. As it requires much too much imagination to find romance in the present, one looks for it in the past, and so a dive is made into some period

[1] Vogue, 1918.

of history, and its monuments studied and copied, and finally "adapted" to the more elaborate exigencies of modern life. But, alas, these divers into the past seem never to have been able to find the pearl of romance, for, ever since the craze began in the eighteenth century, they have been diving now here, now there, now into Romanesque, now into Gothic, now into Jacobean, now into Queen Anne. They have brought up innumerable architectural "features" which have been duly copied by modern machinery, and carefully glued on to the houses, and still the owners and the architects, to do them justice, feel restless, and are in search of some new "old style" to try. The search has flagged of late, people know it is useless, and here and there architects have set to work merely to build so well and with such a fine sense of the material employed that the result should satisfy the desire for comeliness without the use of any style. I am thinking of some of Mr. Blow's earlier works where a peculiar charm resulted from the unstinting care with which every piece of material had been chosen and the whole fitted together almost as though the stones had been precious stones instead of flints or bricks.

But on the whole the problem appears to be still unsolved, and the architects go on using styles of various kinds with greater or less degrees of correctness. This they no longer do with the old zest and hope of discovery but rather with a languid indifference and with evident marks of discouragement.

Now style is an admirable thing, it is the result of ease and coherence of feeling, but unfortunately a borrowed style is an even stronger proof of muddled and befogged emotions than the total absence of style. The desire for a style at all costs, even a borrowed style, is part of that exaggerated social consciousness which in other respects manifests itself as snobbery. What if people were just to let their houses be the direct outcome of their actual needs, and of their actual way of life, and allow other people to think what they like. What if they behaved in the matter of houses as all people wish to behave in society without any undue or fussy self-consciousness. Wouldn't such houses have really a great deal more character, and therefore interest for others, than those which are deliberately made to look like something or other. Instead of looking like something, they would then be something.

The house which I planned and built for myself was the result of certain particular needs and habits. I had originally no idea of building a house: I had so often heard the proverb that "Fools build houses for wise men to live in," that I had come to believe it, but I required a house of a certain size for my family within easy reach of London. I looked at a great many houses and found that those which had a sufficient number of rooms were all gentlemen's establishments, with lodge, stabling, and greenhouses. Now it was characteristic of my purse that I could not afford to keep up a gentleman's establishment and of my tastes that I could not endure to. I was a town dweller, and I wanted a town house and a little garden in the country. As I could not find what I wanted, the idea came into my head that I must build it or go without. The means at my disposal were definitely limited; the question was therefore whether I could build a house of the required size with that sum. I made a plan containing the number of rooms of the sizes I required, and got an estimate. It was largely in excess of the sum I possessed for the purpose. I feared I must give up my scheme when I met a friend who had experimented in building cheap cottages on his estate, and learned from him that the secret of economy was concentration of plan. I also discovered in discussing my first estimate that roofs were cheaper than walls. I thereupon started on a quite different plan, in which I arranged the rooms to form as nearly as possible a solid block, and placed a number of the rooms in a hipped or Mansard roof. It will be seen that, so far, the planning of the house was merely the discovery of a possible equation between my needs and the sum at my disposal.

But in trying to establish this equation I had found it necessary to make the rooms rather smaller than I should have liked, and having a great liking for large and particularly high interiors—I hate Elizabethan rooms with their low ceilings in spite of their prettiness, and I love the interiors of the baroque palaces of Italy— I determined to have one room of generous dimensions and particularly of great height. This large room surrounded by small rooms was naturally made into a general living-place, with arrangements by means of a lift to enable it to be used as a dining hall if there were more in the house than could be accommodated in the small breakfast room.

The estimate for this new concentrated plan, in spite of the large dimensions of the living place, came to little more than half the estimate for the former plan, and made my project feasible, provided that I could calculate all details and did not run into extras.

So far then there has been no question of architecture; it has been merely solving the problem of personal needs and habits, and of cost, and if architecture there is to be, it should, I think, come directly out of the solution of these problems. The size and disposition of the plan having thus been fixed, the elevations are given in outline, and the only question is how the rectangle of each elevation is to be treated. Doors and windows are the elements of the design, and here again something will already be determined by needs or tastes. There is need of a certain amount of light, and my own taste is to have as much as possible, so that the windows had to be large rectangles. But when all these things are determined by need there is still a wide margin of choice—the size of the panes in the windows, the depth of recess of the windows within the wall, the flatness or relief of each element. All these and many more are still matters of choice, and it is through the artist's sense of proportion and his feeling for the plastic relief of the whole surface that a work of mere utility may become a work of art. In the case of the main elevation of my house I found that when all the windows, including the long windows of the high living-place, were duly arranged, there was a want of unity owing to the nearly equal balance between the horizontal and vertical members. I therefore underlined the slight projection of the central part—a projection enforced by by-laws—by varying the material, replacing at this point the plaster of the walls by two bands of red brick. In this way the vertical effect of the central part was made to dominate the whole façade. The artistic or architectural part of this house was confined, then, merely to the careful choice of proportions within certain fixed limits defined by needs, and neither time, money, nor thought was expended on giving the house the appearance of any particular style.

I have gone thus at length into the history of my own house merely as an example of the way in which, I think, a genuine architecture, and in the end, no doubt, an architectural style, might arise. It requires a certain courage or indifference to public opinion on the part of the owner. My own house is neighboured by houses of the most gentlemanly picturesqueness, houses from which tiny gables with window slits jut out at any unexpected angle, and naturally it is regarded as a monstrous eyesore by their inhabitants. Indeed, when I first came here it was supposed that the ugliness of my house was so apparent that I myself could not be blind to it, and should not resent its being criticised in my presence. They were quite right, I did not resent it; I was only very much amused.

To arrive at such a genuine domestic architecture as I conceive, requires, then, this social indifference to surrounding snobbishness on the part of the owner, and it requires a nice sense of proportion and a feeling for values of plastic relief on the part of the artist who designs the house, but it does not require genius or even any extraordinary talent to make a genuine and honest piece of domestic architecture which will continue to look distinguished when the last "style" but one having just become *démodé* already stinks in the nostrils of all cultured people.

JEAN MARCHAND[1]

THERE are some thirty pictures by M. Jean Marchand now on view at the Carfax Gallery in Bury Street. This gives one an occasion for reviewing the work of this comparatively young artist. M. Marchand belongs, of course, to the revolutionary movement of this century in that he derives the general principles of his art from Cézanne, but he is the most traditional of revolutionaries. Not by the wildest stretch of the imagination could one conceive of M. Marchand deliberately or consciously doing anything to astonish the public. It is quite true that no genuine artist ever did, but some artists have found an added piquancy in the thought that inventions that occurred to them would in point of fact have this adventitious charm. But with M. Marchand such possibilities seem more remote than with most of his compeers. An extreme simplicity and directness of outlook and a touching sincerity in all that he does are the most prominent characteristics of his work. Not that he makes one suppose him to be too naïve to play tricks with his art; on the contrary, one sees that he is highly self-conscious and intellectual, but that

[1] Athenæum, 1919.

H

he knows the utter futility of any deliberate emphasis on the artist's part. He knows that any effect of permanent value must flow directly from the matter in hand; that it is useless to make anything appear more interesting or impressive than it is; that, whatever his vision is, it must be accepted literally, and without any attempt to add to its importance or effectiveness.

In short, M. Marchand is a classic artist—one might almost in these days say a French artist, and count it as synonymous, but that one remembers that the French, too, have had their orgies of romantic emphasis, and have always ready to hand a convention of coldly exaggerated rhetoric. Moreover, if one thinks of a nearly allied painter such as Derain, whose work is so terribly *interesting*, one sees that to a quite peculiar degree M. Marchand exemplifies the sentimental honesty of the French. I leave the question open whether this is a moral trait, or is not rather the result of a clearer perception that we often attain to of the extreme futility of lying where art is concerned.

Certainly one can imagine the temptations for a man of M. Marchand's great technical ability to choose some slightly wilful or fantastic formula of vision and to exploit it for what it might bring out; for M. Marchand was handicapped in any competition for notoriety by the very normality and sanity of his vision. Compared to the descriptions of sketches in "Jane Eyre," his pictures would be judged to be entirely lacking in imagination. He never tries to invent what he has not actually seen. Almost any of the ordinary things of life suffice for his theme—a loaf of bread or a hat left on the table, a rather vulgar French château restored by Viollet-le-Duc with a prim garden and decorous lake, a pot of aspidistra in a suburban window. These and the like are the subjects of his pictures, and he paints the objects themselves in all their vulgar everydayness. They do not become excuses for abstract designs; they retain in his pictures all their bleak commonplaceness.

Any one unfamiliar with his pictures who read such an account of his work might think M. Marchand was a dull literalist, whose mere accomplishment it is to render the similitude of objects. But such a conclusion would be entirely wrong. However frankly M. Marchand accepts the forms of objects, however little his normal vision distorts or idealises them, however consciously and deliberately he chooses the arrangement, he does build up by sheer method and artistic science a unity which has a singularly impressive quality. I heard some one say, in front of a still life which represented a white tablecloth, a glass tumbler, an earthenware waterbottle and a loaf of bread, that it was like Buddha. With such a description as I give of the picture the appreciation sounds precious and absurd; before the picture it seems perfectly just. For M. Marchand has attained the reward of his inflexible honesty; his construction is so solid and unfaltering he builds up his designs with such massive and direct handling, that without the slightest suggestion of emphasis, without any underlining, the effect comes through; the material becomes expressive; he becomes a creator, and not a mere adapter of form.

For the understanding of his personality it is interesting to consider his Cubist period, since Marchand's reaction to Cubism is typical of his nature. Cubism, like S. Paul, has been all things to all men—at least to almost all artists of the present generation. To some it has been a doctrine and a revelation; to some it has been a convenient form of artistic journalism; to some it has been a quick road to notoriety, to some an aid to melodramatic effect. To M. Marchand it was just a useful method and a gymnastic. He used it for just what it could give him as an exercise in the organisation of form. It was to him like a system of notation to a mathematician, a means of handling quantities which without it would have been too elusive and too infinite to grasp. By means of Cubism the infinity of a sphere could be reduced to half a dozen planes, each of which he could learn to relate to all the other planes in the picture; and the singular ease and directness of his plastic construction seem to be due to his early practice of Cubist methods. Having once learned by this process of willed and deliberate analysis how to handle complex forms, he has been able to throw away the scaffolding and to construct palpably related and completely unified designs with something approaching the full complexity of natural forms, though the lucid statement and the ease of handling which it actuates testify to the effect of his apprenticeship in Cubism. Such a use of a theory— as a method, not as a doctrine—seems to me typical of M. Marchand's balanced judgment, of his alert readiness to use any and every means that could conduce to his slow and methodical development, and hold out hopes of a continued growth.

M. Marchand, so assured, so settled an artist, is still young. In the landscapes which he did in the South of France just before the war he explored a peculiarly persuasive and harmonious scheme of colour, based on warm ochres, earth reds, and dull blues. These pictures have the envelopment and the sonorous harmony of some early Italian masters in spite of the frank oppositions and the vigorous scaffolding of modern design. In the later work done in the last year he shows a new sense of colour, a new sharpness and an almost audacity, if one can imagine so well-balanced a nature capable of audacity. He uses dull neutral colours, the dirty white of a cloudy sky, harsh dull greens and blacks, the obvious and unattractive colours that so frequently occur in nature; but he uses them in such combinations, and with such accents

of tone and such subtly prepared accordances and
oppositions, that these obvious dull colours strike one
as fascinating discoveries. This is the height of artistic
science, so to accept the obvious and commonplace
that it gives one the pleasant shock of paradox. It
seems hardly rash to foretell for him a solid and continually growing fame.

RETROSPECT [1]

THE work of re-reading and selecting from the mass
of my writings as an art critic has inevitably brought
me up against the question of its consistency and
coherence. Although I do not think that I have
republished here anything with which I entirely disagree, I cannot but recognise that in many of these
essays the emphasis lies in a different place from where
I should now put it. Fortunately I have never prided
myself upon my unchanging constancy of attitude,
but unless I flatter myself I think I can trace a certain
trend of thought underlying very different expressions
of opinion. Now since that trend seems to me to be
symptomatic of modern æsthetic, and since it may
perhaps explain much that seems paradoxical in the
actual situation of art, it may be interesting to
discuss its nature even at the cost of being autobio-
graphical.

In my work as a critic of art I have never been a
pure Impressionist, a mere recording instrument of
certain sensations. I have always had some kind of
æsthetic. A certain scientific curiosity and a desire
for comprehension have impelled me at every stage
to make generalisations, to attempt some kind of
logical co-ordination of my impressions. But, on the
other hand, I have never worked out for myself a
[1] 1920.

complete system such as the metaphysicians deduce
from *a priori* principles. I have never believed that I
knew what was the ultimate nature of art. My æsthetic
has been a purely practical one, a tentative expedient,
an attempt to reduce to some kind of order my æsthetic
impressions up to date. It has been held merely until
such time as fresh experiences might confirm or modify
it. Moreover, I have always looked on my system
with a certain suspicion. I have recognised that if it
ever formed too solid a crust it might stop the inlets
of fresh experience, and I can count various occasions
when my principles would have led me to condemn,
and when my sensibility has played the part of Balaam
with the effect of making temporary chaos of my system.
That has, of course, always rearranged itself to take
in the new experience, but with each such cataclysm
it has suffered a loss of prestige. So that even in its
latest form I do not put forward my system as more
than a provisional induction from my own æsthetic
experiences.

I have certainly tried to make my judgment as
objective as possible, but the critic must work with
the only instrument he possesses—namely, his own
sensibility with all its personal equations. All that
he can consciously endeavour is to perfect that tool
to its utmost by studying the traditional verdicts of
men of æsthetic sensibility in the past, and by constant
comparison of his own reactions with those of his
contemporaries who are specially gifted in this way.
When he has done all that he can in this direction—
and I would allow him a slight bias in favour of agree-
ment with tradition—he is bound to accept the verdict
of his own feelings as honestly as he can. Even plain
honesty in this matter is more difficult to attain than
would be supposed by those who have never tried it.
In so delicate a matter as the artistic judgment one is
liable to many accidental disturbing influences, one

can scarcely avoid temporary hypnotisms and hallucinations. One can only watch for and try to discount these, taking every opportunity to catch one's sensibility unawares before it can take cover behind prejudices and theories.

When the critic holds the result of his reaction to a work of art clearly in view he has next to translate it into words. Here, too, distortion is inevitable, and it is here that I have probably failed most of accuracy, for language in the hands of one who lacks the mastery of a poet has its own tricks, its perversities and habits. There are things which it shies at and goes round, there are places where it runs away and, leaving the reality which it professes to carry tumbled out at the tail of the cart, arrives in a great pother, but without the goods.

But in spite of all these limitations and the errors they entail it seems to me that the attempt to attain objective judgments has not altogether failed, and that I seem to myself to have been always groping my way towards some kind of a reasoned and practical æsthetic. Many minds have been engaged alongside of mine in the same pursuit. I think we may claim that partly as a result of our common efforts a rather more intelligent attitude exists in the educated public of to-day than obtained in the last century.

Art in England is sometimes insular, sometimes provincial. The pre-Raphaelite movement was mainly an indigenous product. The dying echoes of this remarkable explosion reverberated through the years of my nonage, but when I first began to study art seriously the vital movement was a provincial one. After the usual twenty years of delay, provincial England had become aware of the Impressionist movement in France, and the younger painters of promise were working under the influence of Monet. Some of them even formulated theories of naturalism in its most literal and extreme form. But at the same time Whistler, whose Impressionism was of a very different stamp, had put forward the purely decorative idea of art, and had tried in his " Ten o'clock," perhaps too cavalierly, to sweep away the web of ethical questions, distorted by æsthetic prejudices, which Ruskin's exuberant and ill-regulated mind had spun for the British public.

The Naturalists made no attempt to explain why the exact and literal imitation of nature should satisfy the human spirit, and the " Decorators " failed to distinguish between agreeable sensations and imaginative significance.

After a brief period during which I was interested in the new possibilities opened up by the more scientific evaluation of colour which the Impressionists practised, I came to feel more and more the absence in their work of structural design. It was an innate desire for this aspect of art which drove me to the study of the Old Masters and, in particular, those of the Italian Renaissance, in the hope of discovering from them the secret of that architectonic idea which I missed so badly in the work of my contemporaries. I think now that a certain amount of " cussedness " led me to exaggerate what was none the less a genuine personal reaction. Finding myself out of touch with my generation I took a certain pleasure in emphasising my isolation. I always recognised fully that the only vital art of the day was that of the Impressionists whose theories I disbelieved, and I was always able to admit the greatness of Degas and Renoir. But many of my judgments of modern art were too much affected by my attitude. I do not think I ever praised Mr. Wilson Steer or Mr. Walter Sickert as much as they deserved, and I looked with too great indulgence on some would-be imitators of the Old Masters. But my most serious lapse was the failure to discover the genius of Seurat, whose supreme merits as a designer I had every reason to acclaim. I cannot even now tell whether I ever saw his work in the exhibitions of the early nineties, but if I did his qualities were hidden from me by the now transparent veil of pointillism—a pseudo-scientific system of atmospheric colour notation in which I took no interest.

I think I can claim that my study of the Old Masters was never much tainted by archæological curiosity. I tried to study them in the same spirit as I might study contemporary artists, and I always regretted that there was no modern art capable of satisfying my predilections. I say there was no modern art because none such was known to me, but all the time there was one who had already worked out the problem which seemed to me insoluble of how to use the modern vision with the constructive design of the older masters. By some extraordinary ill luck I managed to miss seeing Cézanne's work till some considerable time after his death. I had heard of him vaguely from time to time as a kind of hidden oracle of ultra-impressionism, and, in consequence, I expected to find myself entirely unreceptive to his art. To my intense surprise I found myself deeply moved. I have discovered the article in which I recorded this encounter, and though the praise I gave would sound grudging and feeble to-day —for I was still obsessed by ideas about the content of a work of art—I am glad to see that I was so ready to scrap a long-cherished hypothesis in face of a new experience.

In the next few years I became increasingly interested in the art of Cézanne and of those like Gauguin and van Gogh who at that time represented the first effects of his profound influence on modern art, and I gradually recognised that what I had hoped for as a possible event of some future century had already occurred, that art had begun to recover once more the language of design and to explore its so long neglected possibilities. Thus it happened that when at the end of

1911, by a curious series of chances, I was in a position to organise an exhibition at the Grafton Galleries, I seized the opportunity to bring before the English public a selection of works conforming to the new direction. For purposes of convenience it was necessary to give these artists a name, and I chose, as being the vaguest and most non-committal, the name of Post-Impressionist. This merely stated their position in time relatively to the Impressionist movement. In conformity with my own previous prejudices against Impressionism, I think I underlined too much their divorce from the parent stock. I see now more clearly their affiliation with it, but I was none the less right in recognising their essential difference, a difference which the subsequent development of Cubism has rendered more evident. Of late the thesis of their fundamental opposition has been again enforced in the writings of M. Lhote.

If I may judge by the discussions in the press to which this exhibition gave rise, the general public failed to see that my position with regard to this movement was capable of a logical explanation, as the result of a consistent sensibility. I tried in vain to explain what appeared to me so clear, that the modern movement was essentially a return to the ideas of formal design which had been almost lost sight of in the fervid pursuit of naturalistic representation. I found that the cultured public which had welcomed my expositions of the works of the Italian Renaissance now regarded me as either incredibly flippant or, for the more charitable explanation was usually adopted, slightly insane. In fact, I found among the cultured who had hitherto been my most eager listeners the most inveterate and exasperated enemies of the new movement. The accusation of anarchism was constantly made. From an æsthetic point of view this was, of course, the exact opposite to the truth, and

I was for long puzzled to find the explanation of so paradoxical an opinion and so violent an enmity. I now see that my crime had been to strike at the vested emotional interests. These people felt instinctively that their special culture was one of their social assets. That to be able to speak glibly of Tang and Ming, of Amico di Sandro and Baldovinetti, gave them a social standing and a distinctive cachet. This showed me that we had all along been labouring under a mutual misunderstanding, *i.e.* that we had admired the Italian primitives for quite different reasons. It was felt that one could only appreciate Amico di Sandro when one had acquired a certain considerable mass of erudition and given a great deal of time and attention, but to admire a Matisse required only a certain sensibility. One could feel fairly sure that one's maid could not rival one in the former case, but might by a mere haphazard gift of Providence surpass one in the second. So that the accusation of revolutionary anarchism was due to a social rather than an æsthetic prejudice. In any case the cultured public was determined to look upon Cézanne as an incompetent bungler, and upon the whole movement as madly revolutionary. Nothing I could say would induce people to look calmly enough at these pictures to see how closely they followed tradition, or how great a familiarity with the Italian primitives was displayed in their work. Now that Matisse has become a safe investment for persons of taste, and that Picasso and Derain have delighted the miscellaneous audience of the London Music Halls with their designs for the Russian Ballet, it will be difficult for people to imagine the vehemence of the indignation which greeted the first sight of their works in England.

In contrast to its effect on the cultured public the Post-Impressionist exhibition aroused a keen interest among a few of the younger English artists and their friends. With them I began to discuss the problems of æsthetic that the contemplation of these works forced upon us.

But before explaining the effects of these discussions upon my æsthetic theory I must return to consider the generalisations which I had made from my æsthetic experiences up to this point.

In my youth all speculations on æsthetic had revolved with wearisome persistence around the question of the nature of beauty. Like our predecessors we sought for the criteria of the beautiful, whether in art or nature. And always this search led to a tangle of contradictions or else to metaphysical ideas so vague as to be inapplicable to concrete cases.

It was Tolstoy's genius that delivered us from this *impasse*, and I think that one may date from the appearance of " What is Art ? " the beginning of fruitful speculation in æsthetic. It was not indeed Tolstoy's preposterous valuation of works of art that counted for us, but his luminous criticism of past æsthetic systems, above all, his suggestions that art had no special or necessary concern with what is beautiful in nature, that the fact that Greek sculpture had run prematurely to decay through an extreme and non-æsthetic admiration of beauty in the human figure afforded no reason why we should for ever remain victims of their error.

It became clear that we had confused two distinct uses of the word beautiful, that when we used beauty to describe a favourable æsthetic judgment on a work of art we meant something quite different from our praise of a woman, a sunset or a horse as beautiful. Tolstoy saw that the essence of art was that it was a means of communication between human beings. He conceived it to be *par excellence* the language of emotion. It was at this point that his moral bias led him to the strange conclusion that the value of a work of art corresponded to the moral value of the emotion expressed. Fortunately he showed by an application of his theory to actual works of art what absurdities it led to. What remained of immense importance was the idea that a work of art was not the record of beauty already existent elsewhere, but the expression of an emotion felt by the artist and conveyed to the spectator.

The next question was, Of what kind of emotions is art the expression? Is love poetry the expression of the emotion of love, tragedy the expression of pity and fear, and so forth? Clearly the expression in art has some similarity to the expression of these emotions in actual life, but it is never identical. It is evident that the artist feels these emotions in a special manner, that he is not entirely under their influence, but sufficiently withdrawn to contemplate and comprehend them. My " Essay in Æsthetic " here reprinted, elaborates this point of view, and in a course of unpublished lectures I endeavoured to divide works of visual art according to the emotional point of view, adopting the classification already existing in poetry into Epic, Dramatic, Lyric, and Comedic.

I conceived the form of the work of art to be its most essential quality, but I believed this form to be the direct outcome of an apprehension of some emotion of actual life by the artist, although, no doubt, that apprehension was of a special and peculiar kind and implied a certain detachment. I also conceived that the spectator in contemplating the form must inevitably travel in an opposite direction along the same road which the artist had taken, and himself feel the original emotion. I conceived the form and the emotion which it conveyed as being inextricably bound together in the æsthetic whole.

About the time I had arrived at these conclusions the discussion of æsthetic stimulated by the appearance of Post-Impressionism began. It became evident through these discussions that some artists who were peculiarly sensitive to the formal relations of works of art, and who were deeply moved by them, had almost no sense of the emotions which I had supposed them to convey. Since it was impossible in these cases to doubt the genuineness of the æsthetic reaction it became evident that I had not pushed the analysis of works of art far enough, had not disentangled the purely æsthetic elements from certain accompanying accessories.

It was, I think, the observation of these cases of reaction to pure form that led Mr. Clive Bell in his book, " Art," to put forward the hypothesis that however much the emotions of life might appear to play a part in the work of art, the artist was really not concerned with them, but only with the expression of a special and unique kind of emotion, the æsthetic emotion. A work of art had the peculiar property of conveying the æsthetic emotion, and it did this in virtue of having " significant form." He also declared that representation of nature was entirely irrelevant to this and that a picture might be completely non-representative.

This last view seemed to me always to go too far since any, even the slightest suggestion, of the third dimension in a picture must be due to some element of representation. What I think has resulted from Mr. Clive Bell's book, and the discussions which it has aroused on this point is that the artist is free to choose any degree of representational accuracy which suits the expression of his feeling. That no single fact, or set of facts, about nature can be held to be obligatory for artistic form. Also one might add as an empirical observation that the greatest art seems to concern itself most with the universal aspects of natural form, to be the least pre-occupied with particulars. The greatest artists appear to be most sensitive to those qualities of natural objects which are the least obvious in ordinary life precisely because, being common to all visible objects, they do not serve as marks of distinction and recognition.

With regard to the expression of emotion in works of art I think that Mr. Bell's sharp challenge to the usually accepted view of art as expressing the emotions of life has been of great value. It has led to an attempt to isolate the purely æsthetic feeling from the whole complex of feelings which may and generally do accompany the æsthetic feeling when we regard a work of art.

Let us take as an example of what I mean Raphael's "Transfiguration," which a hundred years ago was perhaps the most admired picture in the world, and twenty years ago was one of the most neglected. It is at once apparent that this picture makes a very complex appeal to the mind and feelings. To those who are familiar with the Gospel story of Christ it brings together in a single composition two different events which occurred simultaneously at different places, the Transfiguration of Christ and the unsuccessful attempt of the Disciples during His absence to heal the lunatic boy. This at once arouses a number of complex ideas about which the intellect and feelings may occupy themselves. Goethe's remark on the picture is instructive from this point of view. "It is remarkable," he says, "that any one has ever ventured to query the essential unity of such a composition. How can the upper part be separated from the lower? The two form one whole. Below the suffering and the needy, above the powerful and helpful—mutually dependent, mutually illustrative."

It will be seen at once what an immense complex of feelings interpenetrating and mutually affecting one another such a work sets up in the mind of a Christian spectator, and all this merely by the content of the picture, its subject, the dramatic story it tells.

Now if our Christian spectator has also a knowledge of human nature he will be struck by the fact that these figures, especially in the lower group, are all extremely incongruous with any idea he is likely to have formed of the people who surrounded Christ in the Gospel narrative. And according to his prepossessions he is likely to be shocked or pleased to find instead of the poor and unsophisticated peasants and fisherfolk who followed Christ, a number of noble, dignified, and academic gentlemen in improbable garments and purely theatrical poses. Again the representation merely as representation, will set up a number of feelings and perhaps of critical thoughts dependent upon innumerable associated ideas in the spectator's mind.

Now all these reactions to the picture are open to any one who has enough understanding of natural form to recognise it when represented adequately. There is no need for him to have any particular sensibility to form as such.

Let us now take for our spectator a person highly endowed with the special sensibility to form, who feels the intervals and relations of forms as a musical person feels the intervals and relations of tones, and let us suppose him either completely ignorant of, or indifferent to, the Gospel story. Such a spectator will be likely to be immensely excited by the extraordinary power of co-ordination of many complex masses in a single inevitable whole, by the delicate equilibrium of many directions of line. He will at once feel that the apparent division into two parts is only apparent, that they are co-ordinated by a quite peculiar power of grasping the possible correlations. He will almost certainly be immensely excited and moved, but his emotion will have nothing to do with the emotions which we have discussed hitherto, since in this case we have supposed our spectator to have no clue to them.

It is evident then that we have the possibility of infinitely diverse reactions to a work of art. We may imagine for instance, that our pagan spectator, though entirely unaffected by the story, is yet conscious that the figures represent men, and that their gestures are indicative of certain states of mind and, in consequence, we may suppose that according to an internal bias his emotion is either heightened or hindered by the recognition of their rhetorical insincerity. Or we may suppose him to be so absorbed in purely formal relations as to be indifferent even to this aspect of the design as representation. We may suppose him to be moved by the pure contemplation of the spatial relations of plastic volumes. It is when we have got to this point that we seem to have isolated this extremely elusive æsthetic quality which is the one constant quality of all works of art, and which seems to be independent of all the prepossessions and associations which the spectator brings with him from his past life.

A person so entirely pre-occupied with the purely formal meaning of a work of art, so entirely blind to all the overtones and associations of a picture like the Transfiguration is extremely rare. Nearly every one, even if highly sensitive to purely plastic and spatial appearances, will inevitably entertain some of those thoughts and feelings which are conveyed by implication and by reference back to life. The difficulty is that we frequently give wrong explanations of our feelings. I suspect, for instance, that Goethe was deeply moved by the marvellous discovery of design, whereby the upper and lower parts cohere in a single whole, but the explanation he gave of this feeling took the form of a moral and philosophical reflection.

It is evident also that owing to our difficulty in recognising the nature of our own feelings we are liable to have our æsthetic reaction interfered with by our reaction to the dramatic overtones and implications. I have chosen this picture of the Transfiguration precisely because its history is a striking example of this fact.

In Goethe's time rhetorical gesture was no bar to the appreciation of æsthetic unity. Later on in the nineteenth century, when the study of the Primitives had revealed to us the charm of dramatic sincerity and naturalness, these gesticulating figures appeared so false and unsympathetic that even people of æsthetic sensibility were unable to disregard them, and their dislike of the picture as illustration actually obliterated or prevented the purely æsthetic approval which they would probably otherwise have experienced. It seems to me that this attempt to isolate the elusive element of the pure æsthetic reaction from the compounds in which it occurs has been the most important advance of modern times in practical æsthetic.

The question which this simile suggests is full of problems; do these form chemical compounds, as it were, in the case of the normal æsthetically gifted spectator, or are they merely mixtures due to our confused recognition of what goes on in the complex of our emotions? The picture I have chosen is also valuable, just at the present time, from this point of view. Since it presents in vivid opposition for most of us a very strong positive (pleasurable) reaction on the purely æsthetic side, and a violently negative (painful) reaction in the realm of dramatic association.

But one could easily point to pictures where the two sets of emotions seem to run so parallel that the idea that they reinforce one another is inevitably aroused. We might take, for instance, Giotto's " Pietà." In my description of that (p. 140), it will be seen that the two currents of feeling ran so together in my own mind that I regarded them as being completely fused. My emotion about the dramatic idea seemed to heighten my emotion about the plastic design. But at present I should be inclined to say that this fusion of two sets of emotion was only apparent and was due to my imperfect analysis of my own mental state.

Probably at this point we must hand over the question to the experimental psychologist. It is for him to discover whether this fusion is possible, whether, for example, such a thing as a song really exists, that is to say, a song in which neither the meaning of the words nor the meaning of the music predominates; in which music and words do not merely set up separate currents of feeling, which may agree in a general parallelism, but really fuse and become indivisible. I expect that the answer will be in the negative.

If on the other hand such a complete fusion of different kinds of emotion does take place, this would tend to substantiate the ordinary opinion that the æsthetic emotion has greater value in highly complicated compounds than in the pure state.

Supposing, then, that we are able to isolate in a work of art this purely æsthetic quality to which Mr. Clive Bell gives the name of " significant form." Of what nature is it ? And what is the value of this elusive and—taking the whole mass of mankind—rather uncommon æsthetic emotion which it causes ? I put these questions without much hope of answering them, since it is of the greatest importance to recognise clearly what are the questions which remain to be solved.

I think we are all agreed that we mean by significant form something other than agreeable arrangements of form, harmonious patterns, and the like. We feel that a work which possesses it is the outcome of an endeavour to express an idea rather than to create a pleasing object. Personally, at least, I always feel that it implies the effort on the part of the artist to bend to our emotional understanding by means of his passionate conviction some intractable material which is alien to our spirit.

I seem unable at present to get beyond this vague adumbration of the nature of significant form. Flaubert's " expression of the idea " seems to me to correspond exactly to what I mean, but, alas! he never explained, and probably could not, what he meant by the " idea."

As to the value of the æsthetic emotion—it is clearly infinitely removed from those ethical values to which Tolstoy would have confined it. It seems to be as remote from actual life and its practical utilities as the most useless mathematical theory. One can only say that those who experience it feel it to have a peculiar quality of " reality " which makes it a matter of infinite importance in their lives. Any attempt I might make to explain this would probably land me in the depths of mysticism. On the edge of that gulf I stop.

WHY BRITAIN IS AT WAR

by

Harold Nicolson

"An admirable summary of the events and policies immediately preceding the present war. It is vigorously written."

C. Delisle Burns in *The Spectator*

"Copies of it should be showered on all neutral countries and presented in bundles to pacifists."

Sir Hugh Walpole in the *Daily Sketch*

A PENGUIN SPECIAL

PELICAN

ARCHÆOLOGY
BELLES LETTRES :
HISTORY : LITERATURE
PSYCHOLOGY : RELIGION

LIGHT BLUE

BOOKS

T : ASTRONOMY

OGY : ECONOMICS

HILOSOPHY : POETRY

IENCE : SOCIOLOGY

PELICAN SPECIALS

*ILLUSTRATED

COVERS

THE
PENGUIN
SHAKESPEARE

EDITED BY G. B. HARRISON

PENGUIN
ILLUSTRATED
CLASSICS

ART DIRECTOR: ROBERT GIBBINGS

BIOGRAPHY
and MEMOIRS

DARK BLUE COVERS

MISCELLANEOUS

YELLOW COVERS

COMPLETE PENGUIN

ARRANGED ALPHABETICALL

For your leisure

moments

FICTION LIST

LOOK FOR THE PENGUIN

ON THE ORANGE COVER

PENGUIN SPECIALS

keeping abreast of

world events :

MYSTERY
and CRIME

PENGUINS HAVE
THE BEST THRILLERS

Look for the PENGUIN on the
GREEN COVER

Adventure & Travel

*illustrated

The Penguins with the
CERISE COVER